THE CRAFTSMAN'S ART SERIES
The Craft of Crochet

The Craftsman's Art Series

The Craft of
Crochet

Pam Dawson

Stanley Paul, London

Stanley Paul & Co. Ltd
3 Fitzroy Square, London W1P 6JD

An imprint of the Hutchinson Publishing Group

London Melbourne Sydney Auckland
Wellington Johannesburg and agencies
throughout the world

First published 1979
© Pam Dawson 1979
Drawings © Stanley Paul & Co. Ltd 1979

Set in Monotype Times

Printed in Great Britain by litho at The Anchor Press Ltd
and bound by Wm Brendon & Son Ltd
both of Tiptree, Essex

British Library Cataloguing in Publication Data
Dawson, Pam
  The craft of crochet.
  1. Crocheting
  I. Title
  746.4′34   TT820

ISBN 0 09 136320 9 cased
       0 09 136321 7 paper

Contents

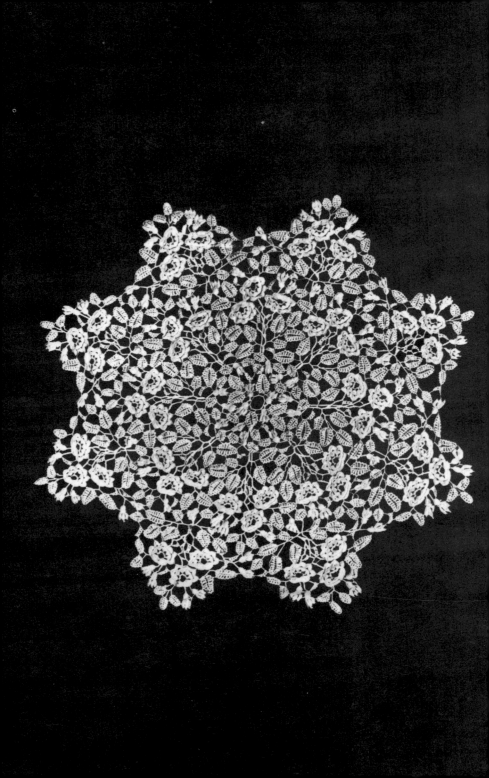

1 An introduction to crochet

I would like to be able to tell you exactly how, when and why crochet first began but, like the invention of the wheel, it is a riddle which cannot be solved. That crochet has survived at all is due in no small measure to the industry of countless generations of nuns, whose skill, inventiveness and cumulative knowledge were only made available to the world outside the cloisters in comparatively recent times, in terms of the overall history of the craft.

Whereas numerous examples of knitting have survived, many pre-dating the Christian era, nothing as tangible remains of crochet. I would put forward the theory that crochet may, in fact, even pre-date knitting. My common sense tells me that it would have been easier for our unknown ancestors to have discovered how to mani-pulate one primitive tool, as opposed to a frame or pair of needles which would be required for knitting – maybe a piece of fish-bone which had an intriguing hook at one end, enabling an inquisitive antediluvian to doodle with a handy length of grass or fibre. But this is mere supposition and I can only give you what few facts I have managed to glean.

The term 'crochet' is derived from the French word *croche*, mean-ing a hook. The craft originally developed as an imitation of lace and, as nuns are known to have been among its first enthusiasts, it is logical to assume that most early examples would have been used for religious embellishments. As the full possibilities of the craft were explored, it deviated from its original form, and stitches and tech-niques which combined both the background fabric and super-imposed embellishments came into use.

By the sixteenth century crochet had outgrown its lace origins and was established as a craft in its own right. From that time on it continued to thrive and one of its loveliest forms, called 'Irish'

Mid-nineteenth century Irish crochet parasol cover
Circular centre with vandyke points added to give a diameter of 61cm
Crown Copyright, Victoria and Albert Museum

Mid-nineteenth century Irish crochet collar and cuffs with vandyke points
Crown Copyright, Victoria and Albert Museum

crochet, had already been developed by the eighteenth century. It is sad to relate that it took the disastrous potato famines in Ireland in the mid nineteenth century to give this craft its greatest impetus. In those terrible times, when thousands were dying of starvation, under the guidance of the nuns every pair of hands – whether they belonged to man, woman or child – had to be employed to make the beautiful crochet lace which was *à la mode* in London at that time. 'Irish' crochet and 'filet' crochet became increasingly popular in Queen Victoria's reign and eventually led to such abuse of these delicate patterns that the craft in general had fallen into disrepute by the beginning of the present century.

It took the very early swing away from our post-war 'plastic' society in the early 1960s to bring crochet back into the position it so rightly deserves. Within a few short years it had been developed and accepted as high fashion, and devotees still continue to explore its full potential as a unique and beautiful craft which is simple in execution and practical in use.

It is the intention of this book to help those who have always wanted to know how to crochet, and to encourage those already proficient in the craft to explore its possibilities. Crochet has several undoubted advantages over knitting: with the exception of Tunisian

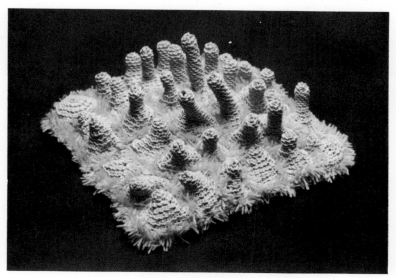

'Sea Urchins'. A wall-hanging showing the modern use of crochet
Designed by Edy Lyngaas

crochet, it requires only one working loop on the hook instead of vast numbers of loops; because of the height of most crochet stitches the fabric grows very quickly; separate crochet motifs are a simple and economical way of using up oddments of yarn and can be joined together to form all types of household items and garments; and, perhaps most important of all, crochet forms a fabric of unusual density and texture which cannot be achieved by any other means.

Probably the most difficult stage for a beginner is learning to control the hook and the yarn. Enthusiasts will also be delighted to find some of the more unusual techniques explained in the following chapters. At every stage care has been taken to explain each step fully and illustrate each movement clearly. Once you begin to discover the scope and enjoyment which this simple craft has to offer, your fingers will itch to experiment.

2 Tools and materials

Unlike many other arts and crafts, very little initial expense is incurred when experimenting with crochet. Because you are creating the fabric and design at one and the same time, you only require a crochet hook and a few balls of yarn to begin your first venture or to extend your knowledge. The craft has three other tremendous advantages. Not one scrap of yarn need ever be wasted: simply unravel, rewind, and you are ready to begin again. You do not need to set aside a specific working area – your crochet can be carried with you wherever you go, to speed up boring train journeys, take your mind off the dentist's waiting-room or simply add to the enjoyment of a sunny afternoon spent in the garden. You do not run the risk of spoiling a particular operation if you have to break off in the middle to rescue an over-active child or answer the telephone – as there is only one working loop on the hook, crochet can be picked up and put down as the fancy takes you.

Apart from hooks and yarn, as you progress in expertise you will find the following items are essential, but most of them will already be available and just need gathering together in a large work bag or box:

A small, sharp pair of scissors
A long, rigid metal rule *or* an unstretchable metric tape measure
A blunt-ended wool sewing needle
A piece of white cotton pressing cloth

Hooks

In the past, hooks were made from bone, ivory, tortoise-shell, steel and plastic. To make the publication of early crochet patterns

Wall-hanging.
Designed by Rosemary Cassidy, Graduate of the Manchester College of Art

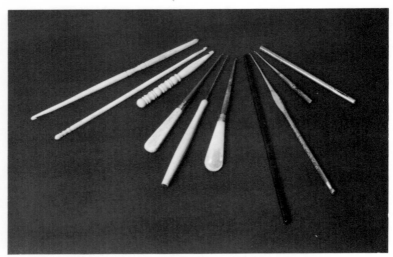

Examples of old hooks

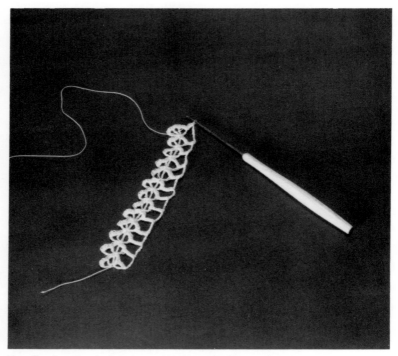

Very fine lace hook showing example worked in sewing cotton

possible, all hooks were eventually graded into wool and cotton sizes in the United Kingdom.

Modern hooks are manufactured from lightweight materials; in Britain and many continental countries they are available in metric sizes, referred to as a number in an 'International Size Range'. This metric figure is based on the exact diameter of the shank of the hook, in millimetres; the larger the metric figure, the greater the diameter of the hook. The chart shows a list of sizes which are available, together with the old wool and cotton sizes. The larger hooks are suitable for heavy yarns and the smaller ones are ideal for fine, delicate work. A beginner would find it easiest to use a medium-sized hook, such as a 4.00.

International Size Range	Old UK Sizes Wool	Cotton
7.00	2	—
—	3	—
6.00	4	—
5.50	5	—
5.00	6	—
4.50	7	—
4.00	8	—
3.50	9	—
3.00	10	3/0
—	11	2/0
2.50	12	0
—	13	1
2.00	14	1½
—	—	2
1.75	15	2½
—	—	3
1.50	16	3½
—	—	4
1.25	—	4½
—	—	5
1.00	—	5½
—	—	6
0.75	—	6½
0.60	—	7
—	—	7½

Crochet hook sizes

Most hooks today from size 0.60 to 1.00 are made from steel, from 1.25 up to 5.00 from anodized aluminium alloy, and from 5.50 upwards from a very high-grade lightweight plastic, which bears the trade name 'Albis' and is referred to as A B S. These materials are of a uniform light grey colour which shows up against any shade of yarn being used and avoids eye strain.

Unlike pairs of needles for knitting, crochet only requires a single hook and, as this holds no stitches, only the working loop, it is

Examples of modern hooks

Example of hook with handle

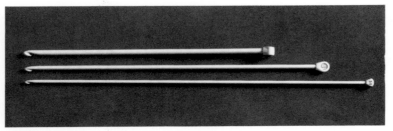

Tunisian hooks

Hairpin prong

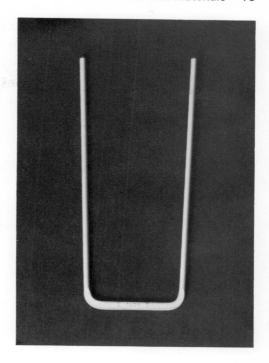

produced to a short length which is easy to manipulate. For those who experience difficulty in holding a hook, sizes 2.00 to 5.00 can be obtained complete with a handle. The exception to this standard length is the type of hook required for Tunisian crochet, where stitches have to be held on the hook. This tool is a combination of a knitting needle and a crochet hook, with a knob at one end and a hook at the other; they are usually made in different lengths such as 30 cm and 35 cm to accommodate varying numbers of stitches. Hairpin crochet also requires a special tool, which is called a 'prong'. This is in the shape of a U and is made to one standard millimetre diameter, with the distance between the vertical portions of the U varying in width from 12 to 80 millimetres.

Yarns

'Yarn' is the overall name given to any spun fibre which is suitable for crochet, whatever its structure, weight or composition. The choice of branded yarns available today is enormous – everything from pure wool and cotton to combinations of natural and man-made fibres.

As you begin to experiment with this craft, however, the range becomes even more exciting. You can spin and dye your own wool, try out ideas using parcel string or roughly textured garden twine, combine a strand of bouclé yarn with a strand of cotton or rayon for an unusual texture.

If you are a complete beginner don't expect to run before you can walk. Stick to a smooth double knitting quality until you become familiar with the basic steps and can manipulate both the hook and the yarn with ease.

Most branded hand-knitting yarns are divided into different categories, such as 4 ply or double knitting, but I want to dispel the mistaken belief that the term 'ply' denotes a yarn of a specific thickness. Each manufactured yarn is made up of single, spun threads and these can be of any thickness. Two, three, four or more single threads are then combined and twisted in various ways to produce the finished yarn. The term '4 ply' is often believed to relate solely to a medium-weight yarn; yet if you unravel an end of double knitting yarn you will more often than not find that this is also made up of 4 plys, with each single thread nearly twice as thick as those used in the construction of a standard 4 ply.

Differences in the texture of yarns are controlled by the way in which the threads are twisted and the combination of fibres used. Yarns which are loosely twisted are lighter and softer to handle than tightly twisted yarns, which are more hard-wearing. As a general guide the following ply classification can be applied to most hand-knitting yarns, whatever their composition.

Baby yarns are made from the highest quality fibres, such as pure botany wool, and are produced in 2, 3, 4 ply and double knitting weights.

Quickerknit yarns are very lightly twisted and are usually equivalent to a standard 4 ply.

2, 3 and 4 ply yarns vary enormously in their construction. Crêpe 4 ply, for instance, is more tightly twisted than a normal 4 ply.

Double knitting yarns are normally double the thickness of standard 4 plys. A double crêpe yarn is more tightly twisted to produce a particularly hard-wearing yarn.

Double double and *chunky yarns* are extra-thick qualities which vary considerably in their construction.

Specialized yarns, such as angora, mohair and lurex qualities, all have completely individual characteristics and cannot normally be placed into a specific ply category.

Crochet coat using hand-spun and hand-dyed wool
Designed by James Walters

When beginning to experiment with crochet an old maxim should apply to the type of fabric you wish to produce, 'Pick the right yarn for the right job.' Don't expect a roughly textured, knobbly tweed yarn to give the best results for fine, lacy work, or a soft, fluffy yarn to produce a rough-and-tumble garment.

Not only does the different character of each yarn determine the type of fabric produced, but the considerable variation in the composition of each yarn can lead to a difference in the total amount required for a project. Because yarn is sold by weight and not length, the content and structure have an effect on the amount in each ball; this can cause problems when trying to substitute another yarn for the specific quality given in a pattern. As an example, pure wool is heavier than pure acrylic, and therefore results in less yardage in each ball of wool. If you pick a pattern which uses acrylic and substitute pure wool, not only will the fabric you obtain be much denser but you will also require more yarn.

3 Tension and turning chains

If you are sufficiently skilled to produce original designs using your own tension, which is based on your control of the hook and yarn, or content to experiment with freehand crochet where the exact size and shape are not of vital importance, you will probably not come up against the important part which 'tension' plays in controlling the finished measurements of a garment. If you eventually intend to work from published crochet patterns, however, this step is so vital that it should really be printed in red ink!

Turning chains also contribute to the neatness of any crochet fabric, both in shaping and final seaming, and their purpose and correct position should be clearly understood before ever beginning to use a hook or yarn.

Tension

The simplest way I can explain the meaning of the word 'tension' is to equate it with an example in dressmaking. A dressmaking pattern tells you exactly how many metres you require of various types of fabrics. It doesn't matter if the pattern calls for chiffon or corduroy, as one metre in width and length are exactly the same. In producing a crochet fabric, however, you are combining the skills of a weaver and dressmaker at one and the same time, and the type of yarn and hook size used mean that the number of stitches and rows required to arrive at a given measurement vary greatly. In a published pattern the number of stitches and rows needed to produce a certain measurement, usually 10 cm, are given under the heading of 'tension'; these were achieved by the original *designer* of the pattern using the specific yarn and hook size quoted. All the eventual calculations for the design were based on these figures.

Humbug floor cushion in Alafoss Lopi wool
Designed by Edy Lyngaas

Once you have mastered the basic steps in crochet you will soon find that it becomes as automatic as breathing, and you will be working in a way which is both natural and comfortable for you. The problem is that everyone varies: there is no such thing as an 'average tension'. Every designer experiences this difference, however slight, and has to begin with a tension sample before working out the instructions for any design. When beginning any pattern, therefore, it is absolutely essential to work a tension sample to make sure that you can achieve the correct number of stitches and rows, otherwise you will end up with a garment which is either much too large or too small.

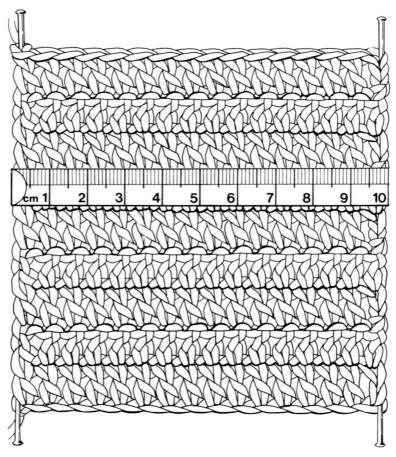

Correct tension sample over 16 trebles and 9 rows

Checking tension

Work a sample using the correct hook size, yarn and stitch given in the pattern, then measure this very accurately with a firm rule. As an example, say a pattern gives a tension of 16 trebles and 9 rows of treble to 10 cm using a size 4.50 hook, make this number of stitches and work the correct number of rows. When you have finished, this sample should measure exactly 10 cm square. Any difference in this measurement means that you have not achieved the correct tension.

If your sample measures *less* than 10 cm then you are working too tightly; to overcome this you should change to one size larger hook and work another sample. If the sample measures *more* than 10 cm then you are working too loosely; you should change to one size

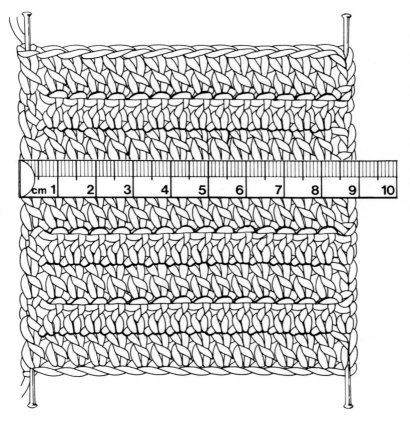

Tension which is too tight over 16 trebles and 9 rows

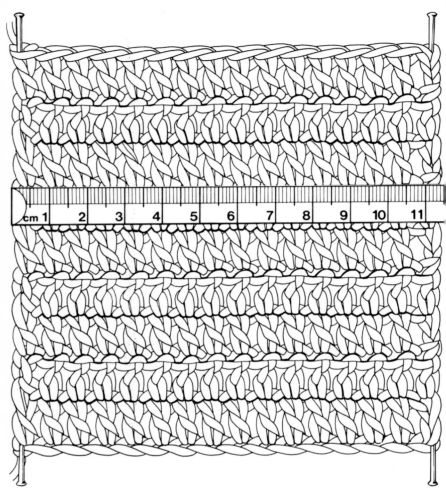

Tension which is too loose over 16 trebles and 9 rows

smaller hook and work another sample. If you can achieve the correct
width but not the exact depth of tension it is usually safe to proceed,
as the length of a garment can be adjusted by working more or less
rows to give the required measurements. In this event, however, do
read right through the pattern to make sure that it is not worked
over an exact number of rows which cannot be adjusted. It doesn't
really matter how many times you have to change hook sizes up or
down in order to achieve the correct tension, but unless you take the

trouble to check this vital point you cannot guarantee that you will achieve perfect results.

Turning chains

This term is so often misunderstood that a few words of explanation at this point will avoid confusion and frustration when attempting your first crochet design.

Quite simply, the row depth of most crochet stitches is considerable, and this is the reason why the work grows so quickly. Because of this it is almost impossible to manoeuvre the hook when working the first stitch of a row. To overcome this difficulty it is necessary to work extra chains at the beginning of a row to bring the hook up to the correct height and these extra chains are referred to as 'turning chains'. The number of extra chains required varies with the stitch being worked. At any time other than when working the first stitch into the commencing chain or unless a specific number of turning chains is quoted in a pattern, the following list is normally used:

Double crochet: 1 or 2 turning chains, according to the thickness of the yarn.
Half treble: 2 turning chains.
Treble: 3 turning chains.
Double treble: 4 turning chains.
Triple treble: 5 turning chains.

The turning chains form the first stitch of a row. To allow for this the first stitch must be missed and the first actual patterned stitch should be worked into the next stitch of the row. Unless the first stitch is missed after working the turning chains you will actually be

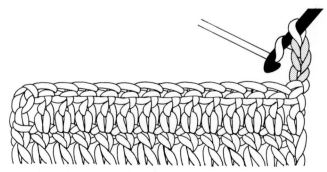

Correct position of turning chains at beginning of row

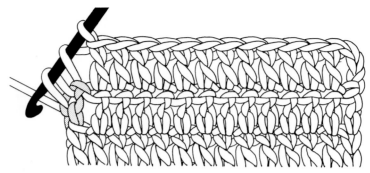

Correct position of last stitch worked into top of turning chain at end of row

increasing a stitch at the beginning of the row. At the end of a row the last patterned stitch is worked into the top of the turning chains which formed the first stitch of the previous row.

These chains not only enable the first stitch in a row to be worked without difficulty but also form a neat edge to the fabric and make seaming easier.

In most published patterns the turning chains are given at the beginning of a row. Some instructions give the number of chains to be worked at the end of the row, before turning the work to commence the next row. Wherever they are worked, the important point to remember is that they take the place of the first stitch of the next row to be worked.

4 Reading crochet instructions

Unless you can pick up a hook and yarn and without any further preamble go straight on to creating your own designs, sooner or later you will come across the peculiar jargon used to indicate certain crochet terms. More often than not beginners fall at this first hurdle and become hopelessly enmeshed in something akin to a foreign language. To be fair to those of us who produce crochet instructions – and perhaps through familiarity sometimes fail to realize just how difficult it is to grasp the written word – you wouldn't really expect to read or speak fluent French without first making some attempt to understand the construction of the language.

Crochet terms and instructions can be written in two entirely different ways, either by means of a form of shorthand in row-by-row instructions, or by means of a series of symbols. The former method is used in the United Kingdom, but continental and American women have become adept at working from a chart where each different stitch is represented by a small symbol. Each method has 'fors' and 'againsts' and it is as well to become familiar with both of them, so that you can decide for yourself which one you prefer.

Written instructions

If a designer has taken exceptional care in producing a beautiful and exciting item, of necessity the instructions will prove rather lengthy. As any publisher will vouch, space in a book or magazine is limited and you very often have to fit all the words plus an illustration into two pages of copy. To overcome this problem a series of standard crochet abbreviations has been devised, and this form of shorthand takes the place of a complete word or term. The list given here covers most of the terms in general use. Where any unusual stitch or technique is employed, the working method is given in full in the instructions when it is first used and then is given an abbreviated form for future use within the pattern.

Do spend some time studying this list. Every comma, asterisk, round or square bracket plays a part in the eventual success of your efforts. If you are a beginner never attempt to read right through a set of instructions as if they were a novel. Have a hook and yarn in your hands so that you can practise each stage, working each little section followed by a comma as a separate manoeuvre before going on to the next step.

List of standard abbreviations used in crochet

alt	alternate(ly)
approx	approximate(ly)
beg	begin(ning)
ch	chain(s)
cl	cluster(s)
cm	centimetre(s)
cont	continu(e)(ing)
dec	decreas(e)(ing)
dc	double crochet
dtr	double treble
foll	follow(ing)
gr	group(s)
grm	gramme(s)
htr	half treble
inc	increas(e)(ing)
patt	pattern
rem	remain(ing)
rep	repeat
RS	right side of work
ss	slip stitch
st(s)	stitch(es)
tog	together
tr	treble
tr tr	triple treble
WS	wrong side of work
yrh	yarn round hook

An asterisk, *, shown in a row indicates that the stitches given after this sign must be repeated from that point as many times as are required to reach the end of the row, or to within the last number of stitches given.

Motivation example: 'Baby's Shawl'
Designed by Phildar Yarns

Instructions contained within square brackets, [ ], or printed in *italics* refer to larger sizes.

Instructions contained within round brackets, ( ), refer to all sizes.

Symbol instructions

The symbol method not only saves considerable space but gives a visual guide to the formation of a pattern or shape. It applies mainly to the actual stitches worked in crochet; where it is used in a set of instructions, the more general terms such as 'decrease' or 'increase' will be given in their abbreviated written form, as in the list.

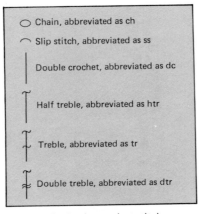

Symbols for basic crochet stitches

Although this method is not very well known in the United Kingdom, it has been in use for very many years. It is believed to have originated in Germany, but I came across a very early example in a Japanese book published in 1865. It is thought that the author of this book was taught how to crochet by a German lady, and although I do not understand Japanese I gather the text is rather quaintly worded, much as Elizabethan English, and gave rise to much mirth when my Japanese colleagues were trying to translate it for me!

General instructions

Any publication dealing with crochet is governed by its own overall format. Some magazines and leaflets give a full stop after each abbreviation, so that double crochet is shown as 'd.c.'. Although this

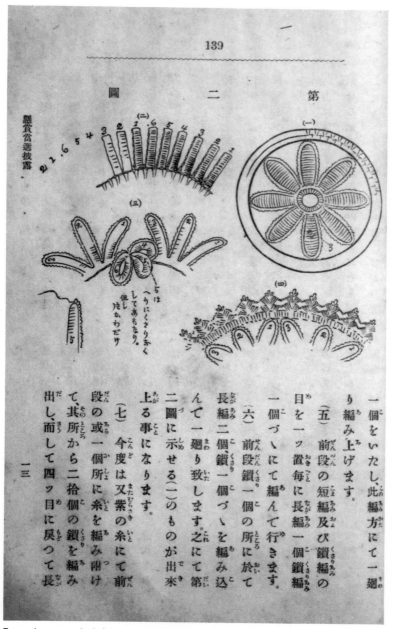

From Japanese knitting text book of 1865 by Mrs H. Toyohara, Department of Home Economics, Kyoritsu Women's University, Tokyo, Japan is strictly correct when giving abbreviations I feel it adds to the confusion and length of instructions and detracts from visual clarity.

Every designer presents their instructions in a different style, and the editor of a magazine or book then has to re-write these to tie in with existing formats. This can be a hazardous stage in producing patterns for publication, as something as simple as a mis-placed comma in a pattern row may make a nonsense of the original design.

In general the first information given in a set of instructions is the finished size of the design, the tension required to produce it and the materials and hook size which the designer has used, although not necessarily in that order. Pay particular attention to this section – if you deviate from the tension or do not use the yarn recommended you cannot blame the publisher for an unsuccessful design.

The design is then split down into sections and given in the order in which they should be worked, such as 'back', 'front', 'sleeves', and so on. If you feel like tackling these sections in a different order do read through first and make sure that the completion of the sleeves doesn't depend on having the back and front available, as is the case with a yoked garment.

The final section deals with the finishing and making up of the item and requires very careful attention. Make sure that the yarn should be pressed before completely ruining all your hard work with a hot iron! Give as much care to joining the seams as you have given to making the fabric. This final attention to detail can make or mar the finished item.

5 How to begin

As a beginner you are probably impatient to work your first few stitches, but do take the trouble to re-read the preceding chapters – it will save you time in the long run!

The first step is to learn how to control and handle the hook and the yarn so that you achieve a continuous, fluid movement and an even fabric.

The instructions and illustrations given in these chapters apply to right-handed people. If you are left-handed the movements are in reverse and you can follow the illustrations if you prop open the book in front of a mirror and work from the reverse image, or lay the book in front of you and work from a pocket mirror placed by the illustrations.

The hook should be held in the right hand and used to form the stitches and the yarn should be wound round the fingers of the left hand to control the flow of the yarn. These illustrations are only intended as a guide and there are no hard-and-fast rules. The important point is to be relaxed and comfortable.

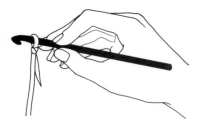

Holding the hook in the right hand

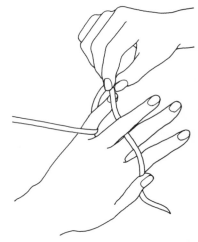

Holding the yarn in the left hand

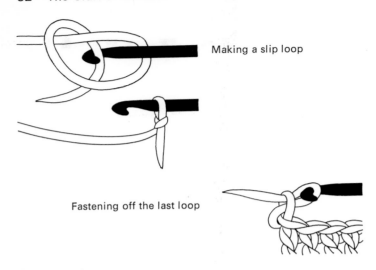

Making a slip loop

Fastening off the last loop

How to begin

All crochet begins with a slip loop on the hook; throughout all stages this loop remains a working loop only and is not counted as a stitch. Once the fabric has been formed this loop still remains on the hook and has to be fastened off securely to complete the section.

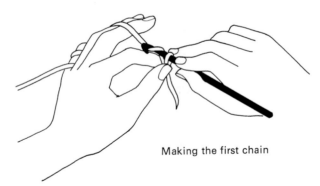

Making the first chain

To work crochet chains

Having formed your first loop you are now ready to make the series of chains which form the foundation of crochet stitches. *Hold the end of yarn below the slip loop between the thumb and index finger

Simple bedspread worked in squares of treble and chains
Designed by Phildar Yarns

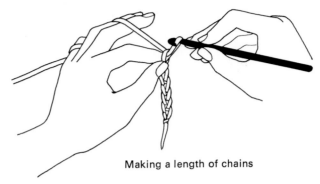

Making a length of chains

of the left hand, use the right hand to place the hook under and over the top of the main end of yarn, which should be held taut over the index and second fingers of the left hand, and catch the yarn in the curve of the hook. This is called 'yarn round hook'. Pull the yarn held in the curve of the hook from the back to the front through the loop on the hook. One chain has been made and the working loop remains on the hook.

Continue in this way from the point marked with an asterisk until the required number of chains have been made, taking care to move the thumb and index finger of the left hand up the chain as it is formed to hold each stitch firmly, and allowing the main yarn to flow freely over the fingers of the left hand.

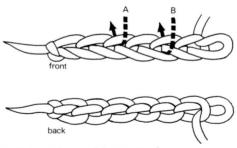

Each chain is made up of 3 strands of yarn

Each chain is made up of three strands of yarn: two strands form the loop which has been pulled through and which remains on the hook; the third is formed by the strand which is carried behind this loop and put round the hook ready to pull through and form the next chain.

When working the first row into this commencing chain to produce a dense fabric, such as treble stitches, a firm edge is achieved by working under the top strand only of the front loop (a). When using an open stitch or one which entails working more than once into the same chain, it is best to go under two of these strands – the top strand of the front loop and the strand across the back of the chain (b).

To work double crochet stitches

Make the number of chains required plus one extra turning chain. Eleven chains form ten double crochet stitches.

Making the first double crochet

1st row. Push the hook through the top loop only of the 3rd chain from the hook from the front to the back, *yarn round hook and draw a loop through the chain (2 loops on hook), yarn round hook and draw through both loops on hook. One double crochet has been made with the 2 missed chains forming the turning chain (see symbols). Push the hook through the top loop of the next chain from the front to the back and repeat from the asterisk. Continue in this way into each chain. At the end of the row turn the work so that the last stitch of this row becomes the first stitch of the next row.

Symbols showing 1st row of double crochet

2nd row. Make 1 chain as the turning chain, miss the first double crochet, *push the hook under both loops at the top of the next double crochet from front to back, yarn round hook and draw a loop

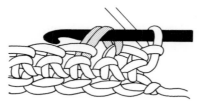

Working under both loops at the top of the double crochet

through (2 loops on hook), yarn round hook and draw through both loops on hook. Continue in this way from the point marked with an asterisk into each double crochet to the last stitch. The last stitch is the turning chain of the previous row and the last double crochet should be worked into the top of this chain. Turn the work.

The 2nd row forms the pattern.

To work half treble stitches

Make the number of chains required, as given for double crochet.

Making the first half treble

1st row. Yarn round the hook, push the hook through the top loop of the 3rd chain from the hook from the front to the back, *yarn round the hook and draw a loop through the chain (3 loops on hook), yarn round the hook and draw through 3 loops on hook. One half treble has been made with the 2 missed chains forming the turning chain (see symbols). Beginning each stitch with yarn round the hook, push the hook through the top of the next chain from front to back and repeat from the asterisk. Continue in this way into each chain. At the end of the row turn as given for double crochet.

Symbols showing 1st row of half trebles

2nd row. Make 2 chains as the turning chain, miss the first half treble, *yarn round the hook, push the hook under both loops at the top of the next half treble from front to back, yarn round hook and draw a loop through (3 loops on hook), yarn round hook and draw through 3 loops on hook. Continue in this way from the point marked with an asterisk into each half treble to the last stitch. The last stitch is the turning chain of the 1st row and the last half treble should be worked into the top of this chain. Turn the work.

The 2nd row forms the pattern.

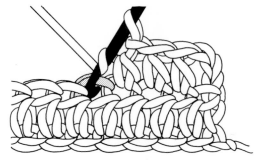

Working under both loops at the top of the half treble

To work treble stitches

Make the number of chains required, plus 2 extra turning chains. 12 chains form 10 treble stitches.

1st row. Yarn round the hook, push the hook through the top loop of the 4th chain from the hook from the front to the back, *yarn round the hook and draw a loop through the chain (3 loops on hook), yarn round the hook and draw through 2 loops on hook (2 loops on hook), yarn round the hook and draw through 2 loops on hook. One treble has been made with the 3 missed chains forming the turning chain (see symbols). Beginning each stitch with yarn round the hook, push the hook through the top loop of the next chain from front to back and repeat from the asterisk. Continue in this way into each chain. At the end of the row turn the work.

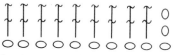

Symbols showing 1st row of treble

2nd row. Make 3 chains as the turning chain, miss the first treble, *yarn round hook, push the hook under both loops at the top of the next treble from front to back, yarn round hook and draw a loop through (3 loops on hook), yarn round hook and draw through 2 loops (2 loops on hook), yarn round hook and draw through 2 loops on hook. Continue in this way from the point marked with an asterisk into each treble to the last stitch. The last stitch is the turning chain of the 1st row and the last treble should be worked into the top of this chain. Turn the work.

The 2nd row forms the pattern.

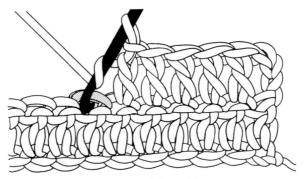

Working under both loops at the top of the treble

To work double treble stitches

Make the number of chains required plus 3 extra turning chains. 13 chains form 10 double treble stitches.

1st row. Yarn round the hook twice, push the hook through the top loop of the 5th chain from the hook from the front to the back, *yarn round the hook and draw a loop through the chain (4 loops on hook), yarn round the hook and draw through 2 loops on the hook (3 loops on hook), yarn round the hook and draw through 2 loops on the hook (2 loops on hook), yarn round the hook and draw through 2 loops on hook. One double treble has been made with the 4 missed chains forming the turning chain (see symbols). Beginning each stitch with yarn round the hook twice, push the hook through the top of the next chain from the front to the back and repeat from the asterisk. Continue in this way into each chain. At the end of the row turn the work.

Symbols showing 1st row of double trebles

2nd row. Make 4 chains as the turning chain, miss the first double treble, *yarn round hook twice, push the hook under both loops at the top of the next double treble from front to back, yarn round hook and draw a loop through (4 loops on hook), yarn round hook and draw through 2 loops on hook, (3 loops on hook), yarn round hook and draw through 2 loops on hook (2 loops on hook), yarn

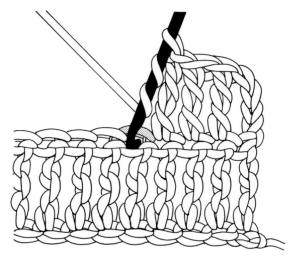

Working under both loops at the top of the double treble

round hook and draw through 2 loops. Continue in this way from the point marked with an asterisk into each double treble to the last stitch. The last stitch is the turning chain of the 1st row and the last double treble should be worked into the top of this chain. Turn the work.

The 2nd row forms the pattern.

More about trebles

Trebles can be further elongated by putting the yarn 3 times round the hook before beginning the stitch and working one more stage than for a double treble to complete the stitch to produce triple trebles; 4 times round the hook before beginning the stitch and working 2 more stages to complete the stitch to produce quadruple trebles, and so on in this way.

To work crochet slip stitches

This is the shallowest of crochet stitches and is seldom used as a pattern. Its main purpose is as a means of getting from one place to another in shaping rows, or as a means of linking the last stitch to the first stitch when working in rounds.

Slip stitches in rows

To work slip stitches along a commencing chain, push the hook through two loops of the 2nd chain from the hook from the front to the back, yarn round the hook and draw through all loops on the hook. One slip stitch has been made. Continue in this way into each chain until the required number of slipped stitches have been worked, slip stitch into the next chain and make the required number of turning chains to begin the first row.

To work slip stitches along a pattern row, miss the first stitch as the loop on the hook compensates for this, push the hook under both loops at the top of the next stitch from front to back, yarn round the hook and draw a loop through the stitch and the loop on the hook. Continue in this way into each stitch until the required number of slipped stitches have been worked, slip stitch into the next stitch, make the required number of turning chains to form the first stitch then continue in pattern to the end of the row.

Working slip stitch in rows

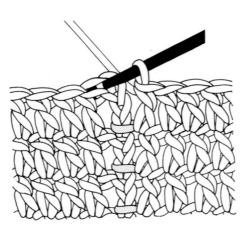

Using slip stitch to join the
last stitch to the first stitch

Using slip stitch
to make a circle

Slip stitch in rounds

To begin a round make the exact number of chains required. To join the chains to form a circle, push the hook through 2 loops of the first chain made, yarn round the hook and draw through all loops on hook.

To join the last stitch to the first in a round, complete the last patterned stitch, push the hook through 2 loops at the top of the turning chain or under both loops at the top of the first stitch of the round, yarn round hook and draw through all loops on hook.

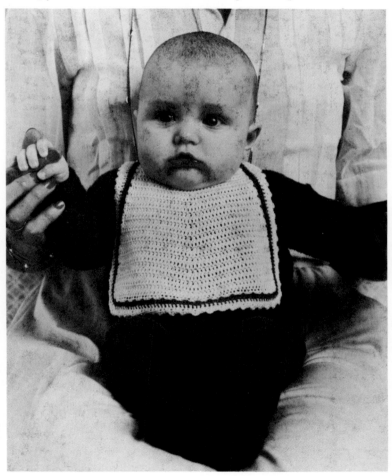

Baby's bib worked in trebles
Designed by Phildar Yarns

6 Working in rows and shaping

Once the basic stitches have been mastered they can be combined and arranged to form patterns which produce different types of all-over fabric. These patterns fall into various groups, such as 'arch' or 'bobble', and range from very open and lacy to dense and three-dimensional effects.

Multiples of stitches

In most instances these patterns still require a turning chain to commence each row, but the initial number of commencing chains is also governed by set multiples of stitches, plus additional edge stitches, to ensure that the pattern works out exactly. In each of the examples shown here the multiples of commencing chains required to establish the pattern are given, so that the fabric can be adjusted to any width.

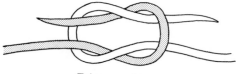

Tying a reef knot

Joining in yarn

Once you begin to make an area of fabric you need to know how to join in a new ball of yarn correctly. When you are working in rows, the new ball should be joined in at the beginning of a row by means of a reef knot. To do this, pass the end of the old ball from left to right over and under the end of the new ball, then take the same end

Cubist jersey in three colours in Jaeger Spiral-spun
Designed by Pam Dawson

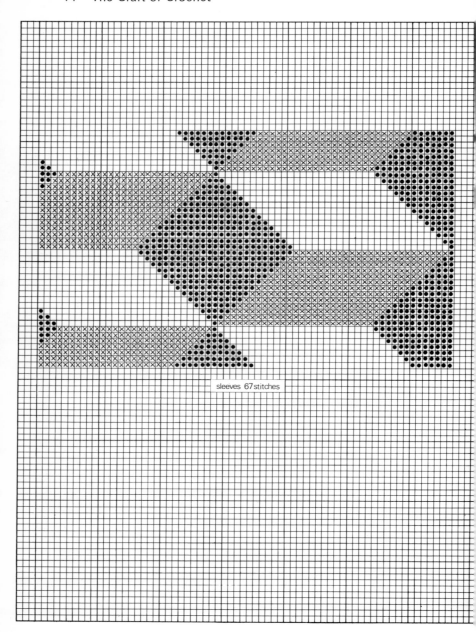

sleeves 67 stitches

Pattern for cubist jersey illustrated on previous page

front and back

□ A light
× B medium
● C dark

77 stitches

from right to left over and under the other end to form a knot. When the section is completed the reef knot can be tightened up and the ends darned in at the edges before beginning to seam. This method should also be used when the yarn cannot be unravelled.

Splicing ends of yarn

Where a new ball is required in the middle of the fabric, as would be the case when working in rounds, the ends of the old and new balls should be spliced together. Unravel the ends of each ball and cut away approximately 10 cm of half of the number of strands in each ball. As an example, on a yarn which has four separate strands, cut away two of these. Overlay the ends which remain from opposite directions and twist them firmly together so that they are of the same thickness as the original yarn. Work the next few stitches very carefully with the newly twisted yarn, then trim away any odd ends.

When working multi-coloured patterns each new colour should be brought into use by working the last stitch of the old colour until 2 loops remain on the hook, make a slip loop with the new colour and place it on the hook then draw this through the 2 loops to complete the stitch and continue working with the new colour. This ensures that the change of colour does not distort the stitch.

Shaping fabric

The width of crochet fabric can be adjusted by increasing or decreasing stitches as directed but, because of the depth of the rows, all shaping must be neatly executed. Merely missing stitches to decrease leaves an ugly gap in the fabric, and seaming becomes difficult if stitches are increased at the extreme edges. Extra chains should be made for large multiples of increased stitches and slip stitches should be used to decrease multiples of stitches.

Increasing stitches

To increase one stitch at each end of a row, work the required number of turning chains at the beginning of the row but instead of missing the first stitch, work into this stitch to increase one. Con-

Bringing in a new colour

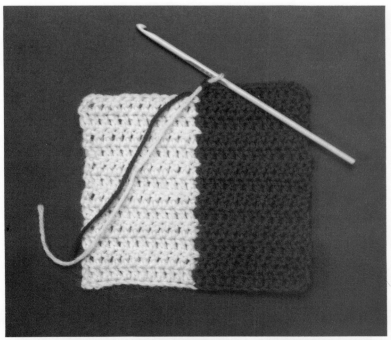

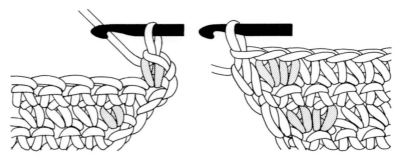

Increasing at each end of a row

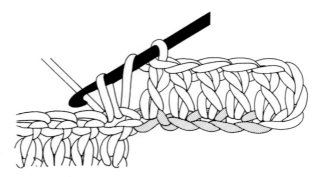

Increasing by means of extra chains at the beginning of a row

tinue in pattern until 2 stitches remain, work twice into the next stitch to increase one, then work the last stitch into the turning chain in the usual way.

Large numbers of stitches can be increased at the beginning of a row by making a chain equivalent to one less than the full number of extra stitches required plus the correct number of turning chains. As an example, if working in trebles where 6 extra stitches are required, make 5 extra chains plus 3 turning chains, 8 in all, work the first treble for the new row into the 4th chain from the hook, then work 1 treble into each of the next 4 chains. The position of the turning chain is now at the beginning of the increased stitches.

Large numbers of stitches can be increased at the end of a row by making a separate length of chains for the exact number of stitches required in the correct yarn. These chains should be joined with a slip stitch to the top of the first stitch of the last row worked, then work in pattern to the end of the row, working one stitch into each of the extra chains to complete the row.

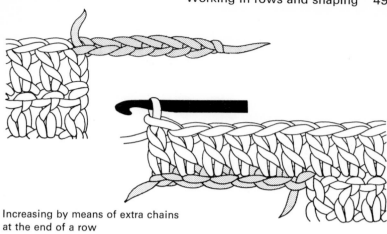

Increasing by means of extra chains
at the end of a row

Decreasing stitches

To decrease one stitch at each end of a row, work the required number of turning chains at the beginning of the row and miss the first stitch, work the next stitch until 2 loops remain on the hook then work the next stitch also until 2 loops remain on the hook, yarn round hook and draw through all loops on hook. The 2 stitches have been drawn together at the top to form one stitch. Continue in pattern until 3 stitches remain, work the next 2 stitches together, then work the last stitch into the turning chain in the usual way.

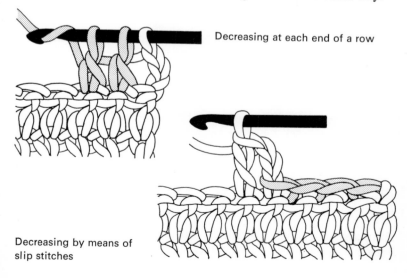

Decreasing at each end of a row

Decreasing by means of
slip stitches

To decrease a large number of stitches at the beginning of a row, slip stitch across the number of stitches to be decreased and into the next stitch. Make the number of chains required for the turning chain, then continue in pattern to the end of the row, noting that the position of the turning chain has been altered. Stitches can be decreased at the end of a row by turning and leaving the required number of stitches unworked.

Arch patterns

These are produced by making chains between each stitch to form a chain-linked effect. Picot mesh is one of the traditional net background stitches used in Irish crochet and in this form is referred to as a 'filling'.

Picot mesh stitch

This requires a number of chains divisible by 4, plus 1 and 5 additional turning chains, e.g. 18 chains.

1st row (RS). Into 10th ch from hook work 1dc, 3ch, 1dc into same ch as before, *5ch, miss 3ch, work (1dc, 3ch, 1dc) into next ch – called 1 picot –, rep from * to last 4ch, 5ch, miss 3ch, 1dc into last ch. Turn.

2nd row. 5ch, work 1 picot into 3rd of first 5ch loop, *5ch, 1 picot into 3rd of next 5ch loop, rep from * to last 9ch loop, 5ch, 1 picot into 3rd of last 9ch loop, 2ch, miss 2ch, 1tr into next ch. Turn.

3rd row. 6ch, *work 1 picot into 3rd of next 5ch loop, 5ch, rep from * to last 5ch loop, 1 picot into 3rd of last 5ch loop, 5ch, 1dc into 3rd of first 5ch. Turn.

4th row. 5ch, work 1 picot into 3rd of first 5ch loop, *5ch, 1 picot into 3rd of next 5ch loop, rep from * to last 6ch loop, 5ch, 1 picot into 3rd of last 6ch loop, 2ch, 1tr into next ch. Turn.

The 3rd and 4th rows form the pattern.

Looped mesh stitch

This requires a number of chains divisible by 4, plus 1 and 4 additional turning chains, e.g. 17 chains.

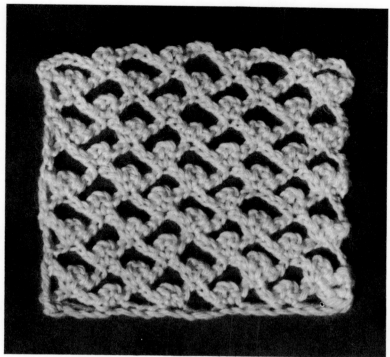

Sample of Picot mesh stitch

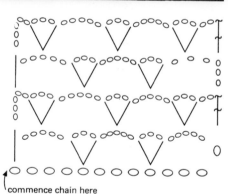

Symbols for Picot mesh stitch   ⌐commence chain here

1st row (RS). Into 7th ch from hook work 1dc, 2ch, miss 1ch, 1tr into next ch, *2ch, miss 1ch, 1dc into next ch, 2ch, miss 1ch, 1tr into next ch, rep from * to end. Turn.

2nd row. 2ch to count as first dc, miss first tr, *3ch, 1dc into next tr, rep from * to end, working last dc into 4th of first 6ch. Turn.

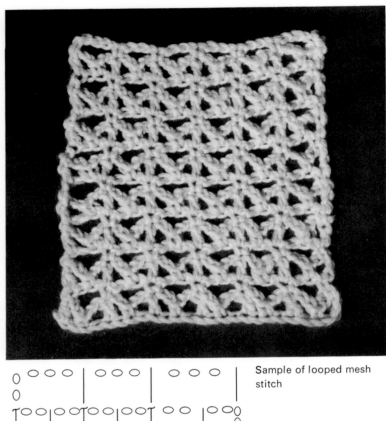

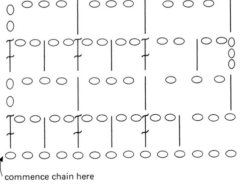

Sample of looped mesh stitch

Symbols for looped mesh stitch

commence chain here

3rd row. 3ch to count as first tr, *2ch, 1dc into 2nd of next 3ch loop, 2ch, 1tr into next dc, rep from * to end, working last tr into 2nd of first 2ch. Turn.

4th row. As 2nd but working last dc into 3rd of first 3ch.

The 3rd and 4th rows form the pattern.

Sample of simple shell stitch

Symbols for
simple shell
stitch

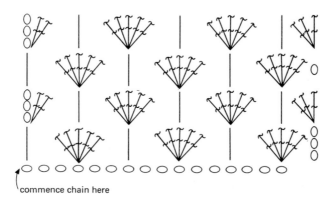

commence chain here

Shell patterns

These are produced by working groups of stitches into a given stitch
in a row to form a fan effect.

Simple shell stitch

This requires a number of chains divisible by 6, plus 1, e.g. 19 chains.

1st row (RS). Into 4th ch from hook work 5tr, *miss 2ch, 1dc into next ch, miss 2ch, 5tr into next ch – called 1 shell –, rep from * to last 3ch, miss 2ch, 1dc into last ch. Turn.

2nd row. 3ch to count as first tr, 2tr into first dc (edge st), *1dc into 3rd of next 5tr, 5tr into next dc, rep from * to last shell, 1dc into 3rd of last 5tr, 3tr into 3rd of first 3ch. Turn.

3rd row. 1ch to count as first dc, * 5tr into next dc, 1dc into 3rd of next 5tr, rep from * to end, working last dc into 3rd of first 3ch. Turn.

4th row. As 2nd but working last 3tr into first 1ch.

The 3rd and 4th rows form the pattern.

Open shell stitch

This requires a number of chains divisible by 10, plus 1 and 5 additional turning chains, e.g. 26 chains.

1st row (RS). Into 6th ch from hook work 1tr, *3ch, miss 3ch, work 1dc into each of next 3ch, 3ch, miss 3ch, work (1tr, 3ch, 1tr) into next ch, rep from * to end, ending with (1tr, 2ch, 1tr) into last ch. Turn.

2nd row. 3ch to count as first tr, 3tr into first 2ch loop, *3ch, 1dc into 2nd of 3dc, 3ch, 7tr into next 3ch loop between tr – called 1 shell –, rep from * to end, ending with 4tr into space between first tr and turning ch. Turn.

3rd row. 1ch to count as first dc, 1dc into each of next 3tr, * 5ch, 1dc into each of next 7tr, rep from * to last shell, 5ch, 1dc into each of next 3tr, 1dc into 3rd of first 3ch. Turn.

4th row. 1ch to count as first dc, 1dc into next dc, *3ch, work (1tr, 3ch, 1tr) into 3rd of next 5ch, 3ch, miss 2dc, 1dc into each of next 3dc, rep from * to end, ending with miss 2dc, 1dc into next dc, 1dc into first 1ch. Turn.

5th row. 1ch to count as first dc, * 3ch, 7tr into next 3ch loop between tr, 3ch, 1dc into 2nd of 3dc, rep from * to end, working last dc into first 1ch. Turn.

Sample of open shell stitch

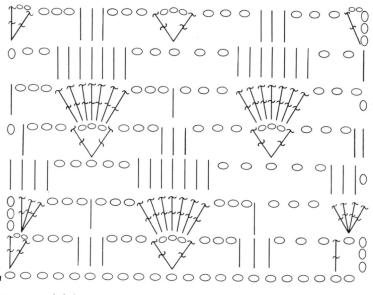

commence chain here

Symbols for open shell stitch

6th row. 1ch to count as first dc, 2ch, *1dc into each of next 7tr, 5ch, rep from * to last shell, 1dc into each of next 7tr, 2ch, 1dc into first 1ch. Turn.

7th row. 3ch to count as first tr, 2ch, 1tr into first dc (edge st), *3ch, miss 2dc, 1dc into each of next 3dc, 3ch, work (1tr, 3ch, 1tr) into 3rd of next 5ch, rep from * to end, ending with (1tr, 2ch, 1tr) into first 1ch. Turn.

The 2nd to 7th rows form the pattern.

Bobble and cluster patterns

These are produced by working more than once into a given stitch in a row, then completing the stitch until only one loop remains to form a clustered effect.

Simple bobble stitch

This requires a number of chains divisible by 4, plus 1 and 1 additional turning chain, e.g. 18 chains.

1st row (RS). Into 3rd ch from hook work 1dc, 1dc into each ch to end. Turn.

2nd row. 1ch to count as first dc, miss first dc, 1dc into next dc, *(yrh, insert hook into next dc and draw up a loop) 5 times into same dc, yrh and draw through 10 loops on hook, yrh and draw through 2 loops on hook – called B1 –, 1dc into each of next 3dc, rep from * to last 3dc, B1, 1dc into next dc, 1dc into 2nd of first 2ch. Turn.

3rd row. 1ch to count as first dc, miss first dc, 1dc into each st to end, working last dc into first 1ch. Turn.

4th row. 1ch to count as first dc, miss first dc, *1dc into each of next 3dc, B1 into next dc, rep from * to last 4dc, 1dc into each of next 3dc, 1dc into first 1ch. Turn.

5th row. As 3rd.

6th row. As 2nd but ending with 1dc into first 1ch.

The 3rd to 6th rows form the pattern.

Sample of simple bobble stitch

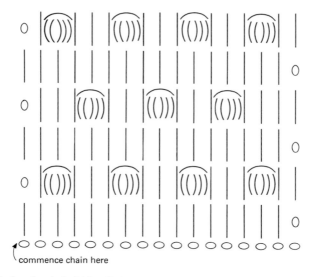

commence chain here

Symbols for simple bobble stitch

Sample of cluster stitch

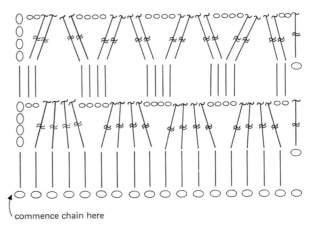

commence chain here

Symbols for cluster stitch

Cluster stitch

This requires a number of chains divisible by 4, plus 2 and 1 additional turning chain, e.g. 19 chains.

1st row (RS). Into 3rd ch from hook work 1dc, 1dc into each ch to end. Turn.

2nd row. 4ch to count as first dtr, 2ch, * keeping last loop of each st on hook work 1dtr into each of next 4dc, yrh and draw through all 5 loops on hook – called 1 cluster –, 4ch, rep from * to last 5dc, work 1 cluster over next 4dc, 2ch, 1dtr into 2nd of first 2ch. Turn.

3rd row. 1ch to count as first dc, 1dc into each of next 2ch, * miss 1 cluster, 1dc into each of next 4ch, rep from * to end, ending with miss 1 cluster, 1dc into each of next 2ch, 1dc into 4th of first 4ch. Turn.

4th row. As 2nd but working last dtr into first 1ch.
 The 3rd and 4th rows form the pattern.

7 Working in rounds

This method can be used to produce separate motifs of almost any shape and size, or a tubular fabric without seams. In each case, unless otherwise stated in a pattern, the work is not turned at the end of a round so the right side of the fabric is always facing you and even something as simple as basic treble stitches have a completely different appearance to when worked in rows.

Tubular fabrics

Begin by making the number of chains required to give the total circumference. Take care to see that the chains do not become twisted and join them into a circle by means of a slip stitch (page 39). Any basic stitch can be used to form the fabric, working the required number of turning chains to begin the round and missing the first chain, then working one stitch into each chain to the end of the round. Join with a slip stitch to the top of the turning chain. Do not turn but continue working in rounds in this way.

Tubular chevron fabric

Tubular fabric can be shaped just as when working in rows (page 43), and new colours can also be brought into use as and when needed. This simple pattern is an ideal way of using up oddments of yarn of the same thickness to form colourful soft toys, draught excluders, stoles or circular cushions.

Make a number of chains divisible by 10, e.g. 50 chains. Join with an ss to first ch to form a circle.

1st round. 3ch to count as first tr, *work 3tr into next ch, 1tr into each of next 3ch, keeping last loop of each st on hook work 1tr into

Detail of tablecloth worked in square and circular motifs   (See p.69)
Designed by J & P Coats

Working tubular fabrics in trebles   Tubular chevron fabric

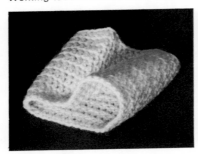 

Chevron cushion in Phildar Pegase
Designed by Pam Dawson

each of next 3ch, yrh and draw through all 4 loops on hook – called 3tr tog –, 1tr into each of next 3ch, rep from * to last 9ch, 3tr into next ch, 1tr into each of next 3ch, 3tr tog, 1tr into each of last 2ch. Join with a ss to 3rd of first 3ch and ss into top of next tr.

2nd round. 3ch to count as first tr, *work 3tr into next tr, 1tr into each of next 3tr, work 3tr tog, 1tr into each of next 3tr, rep from * to end, ending last rep with 1tr into each of last 2tr. Join with a ss to 3rd of first 3ch and ss into top of next tr.

The 2nd round forms the pattern and colours can be changed as required; see pages 46–47 for bringing in new colours correctly.

Motifs worked in rounds

The different motifs which can be produced by this method are almost too numerous to count – anything from the simple but colourful 'granny' square to an intricate Irish crochet motif. Although these motifs are worked in rounds, they produce a flat fabric working outwards from the centre, so provision must be made for increasing in every round, either by means of additional stitches or chain loops between groups of stitches.

Granny squares

These cheerful motifs have endless uses and can be worked to any size in as many colours as you have available. All you need to know is how to work chains, trebles and joining with a slip stitch.

Make 6ch and join with a ss to the first ch to form a circle.

1st round. 3ch to count as first tr, 2tr into circle working under the commencing ch, 2ch, (3tr into circle, 2ch) 3 times. Join with a ss to 3rd of first 3ch. Break off yarn and fasten off.

2nd round. Join next colour to any 2ch space with a ss, 3ch to count as first tr, work 2tr into same space, *1ch, (3tr, 2ch, 3tr) into next space for corner, rep from * twice more, 1ch, 3tr into same 2ch space

Granny square in 4 colours

as beg of round, 2ch. Join with a ss to 3rd of first 3ch. Break off yarn and fasten off.

3rd round. Join next colour to any 2ch space with a ss, 3ch to count as first tr, work 2tr into same space, *1ch, 3tr into next 1ch space, 1ch, (3tr, 2ch, 3tr) into corner 2ch space, rep from * twice more, 1ch, 3tr into next 1ch space, 1ch, 3tr into same 2ch space as beg of round, 2ch. Join with a ss to 3rd of first 3ch. Break off yarn and fasten off.

4th round. Join next colour to any 2ch space with a ss, 3ch to count as first tr, work 2tr into same space, *(1ch, 3tr into next 1ch space) twice, 1ch, (3tr, 2ch, 3tr) into corner 2ch space, rep from * twice more, (1ch, 3tr into next 1ch space) twice, 1ch, 3tr into same 2ch space as beg of round, 2ch. Join with a ss to 3rd of first 3ch. Break off yarn and fasten off.

Darn in all ends on WS of work. You can continue working in this way, increasing one chain and one group of 3 trebles along each side of the square on every round, to give any size.

Cluster motif

This lovely motif has the added advantage of being joined together on the last working round to avoid seaming the motifs.

Make 4ch and join with a ss to first ch to form a circle.

1st round. 1ch to count as first dc, work 7dc into circle working under the commencing ch. Join with a ss to first ch. 8dc.

Cluster motifs joined together

2nd round. 4ch to count as first dtr, work 5dtr into first dc, remove hook from working loop and insert it into the top of the first 4ch, re-insert hook into working loop and draw through st on hook, 2ch, * work 6dtr into next dc, remove hook from working loop and insert it into top of the first dtr, re-insert hook into working loop and draw through st on hook – called 1 cluster –, 2ch, rep from * 6 times more. Join with a ss to top of the first cluster.

3rd round. Ss into first ch space, 3ch to count as first tr, 2tr into same space, 2ch, * 3tr into next ch space, 2ch, rep from * 6 times more. Join with a ss to 3rd of first 3ch.

4th round. 3ch to count as first tr, 1tr into same place, 1tr into next tr, 2tr into next tr, 2ch, * 2tr into next tr, 1tr into next tr, 2tr into next tr, 2ch, rep from * 6 times more. Join with a ss to 3rd of first 3ch.

5th round. 3ch to count as first tr, leaving last loop of each st on hook work 1tr into each of next 4tr, yrh and draw through all loops on hook, * 3ch, 1dc into next ch space, 3ch, 1tr into each of next 5tr, 3ch, 1dc into next ch space, 3ch, leaving last loop of each st on hook work 1tr into each of next 5tr, yrh and draw through all loops on hook – called 1 cluster –, rep from * twice more, 3ch, 1dc into next ch space, 3ch, 1tr into each of next 5tr, 3ch, 1dc into next ch space, 3ch. Join with a ss into top of first cluster.

6th round. 5ch, 1tr into next dc, 5ch, 1 cluster into next 5tr, 5ch, ss into top of last cluster – called 1 picot –, * 5ch, 1tr into next dc, 5ch, 1dc into top of next cluster, 5ch, 1tr into next dc, 5ch, work cluster and picot into next 5tr, *, rep from * twice more, 5ch, 1tr into next dc, 5ch. Join with a ss to first ch. Fasten off.

To join motifs

Work another motif as given for first 5 rounds.

6th round (joining). Work as 6th round from beg to second * omitting last picot, with WS facing place 2nd motif against 1st motif, 1ch, ss into corner picot of 1st motif, ss into top of cluster just completed on 2nd motif, 2ch, ss into next ch space of 1st motif, 2ch, 1tr into next dc on 2nd motif, 2ch, ss into next ch space of 1st motif, 2ch, 1dc into top of next cluster on 2nd motif, 2ch, ss into next ch space of 1st motif, 2ch, 1tr into next dc on 2nd motif, 2ch, ss into next ch space of 1st motif, 2ch, work a cluster into next 5tr of 2nd motif, 1ch, ss into next corner picot of 1st motif, ss into top of cluster just completed on 2nd motif, complete round as given for 1st motif.

Irish crochet rose motif

Irish crochet locket motif
worked in sewing cotton
Designed by J & P Coates

Irish crochet rose

Of all the lovely motifs, or 'sprigs' as they are correctly called in Irish crochet, the rose is the most popular. In traditional Irish crochet sprigs in various shapes and sizes are completed first, then joined together to form an all-over fabric by means of a net background, or 'filling'.

Coil the end of yarn 3 or 4 times round a finger, remove this ring and secure it with a ss.

1st round. 2ch to count as first dc, work 17dc over the coil of yarn. Join with a ss to the 2nd of the first 2ch to form a circle. 18dc.

2nd round. 6ch, miss 2dc, 1htr into next dc, * 4ch, miss 2dc, 1htr into next dc, rep from * 3 times more, 4ch, miss 2dc. Join with a ss to 2nd of first 6ch. 6 loops.

3rd round. Into each 4ch loop work (1dc, 1htr, 3tr, 1htr, 1dc). Join with a ss to top of first dc. 6 petals.

4th round. Ss into back of nearest htr of 2nd round, * 5ch, hold this ch behind petal of 3rd round and ss into back of next htr of 2nd round, rep from * 5 times more, working last ss into same htr as first ss.

5th round. Into each 5ch loop work (1dc, 1htr, 5tr, 1htr, 1dc). Join with a ss to top of first dc.

6th round. Ss into back of ss of 4th round, * 6ch, hold this ch behind petal of 5th round and ss into back of next ss on 4th round, rep from * 5 times more, working last ss into same ss as first ss.

7th round. Into each 6ch loop work (1dc, 1htr, 7tr, 1htr, 1dc). Join with a ss to top of first dc. Fasten off.

Irish crochet table mat
*Designed by
J & P Coats*

Tablecloth worked in squ
and circular motifs
(See p.60 for detail)
Designed by J & P Coat

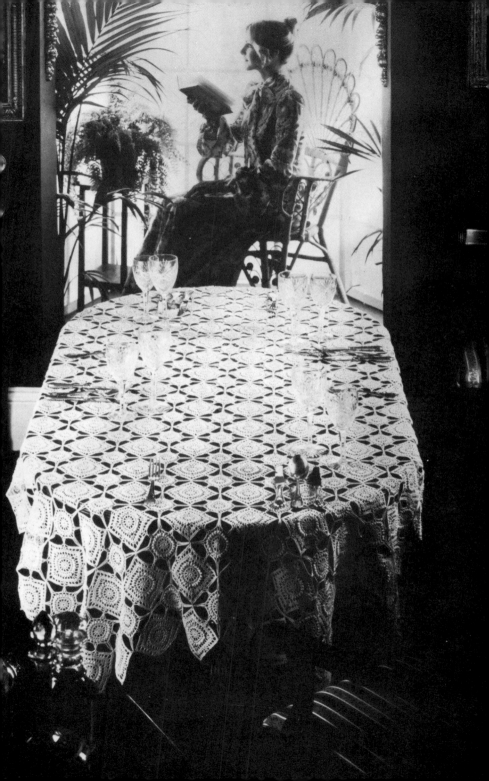

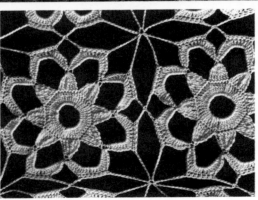

Bedspread worked in motifs
Designed by J & P Coats

Nineteenth century Irish crochet collar
Crown copyright, Victoria and Albert Museum

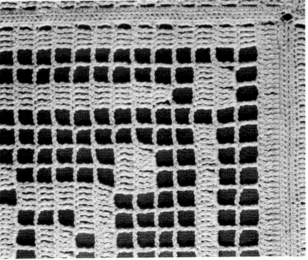

Filet crochet cushion
Designed by J & P Coats

8 Filet crochet

Traditional filet crochet produces a flat fabric comprised of areas of solid patterns linked together by a net background. Only three basic stitches are used – chains, double crochet and trebles. The solid areas are referred to as 'blocks' and are produced by working groups of trebles. The net background is achieved by making two chains linked together by a single treble for each space and these are referred to as 'spaces'. 'Lacets' and 'bars' are also used in this type of crochet to give a lace effect. These four methods are all represented by a different symbol and any pattern can easily be followed from a chart.

Filet crochet is worked in rows, and the beginnings and endings of the rows can be increased or decreased to shape a design, either by single or multiple groups of stitches.

The word 'filet' means 'net' and this background type of fabric has numerous uses. A single row can be worked and threaded with ribbon to form a decorative edging. An all-over area of net can be made and then filled in by looping separate cut ends of yarn into each space to produce a very warm and hard-wearing fabric. Alternatively, lengths of contrasting coloured yarn can be threaded through each of the spaces to form colourful woven fabrics.

How to work blocks

A block is usually made up of 3 trebles and is shown as a cross, 'x', or circle, 'o', on the chart. When 1 block stands alone in the pattern it consists of 4 trebles, the first of which belongs to the previous space. When 2 blocks stand alone there are 7 trebles in the group, 3 for each of the 2 blocks and 1 for the previous space. The simplest method of remembering this formula is to calculate 3 times as many trebles as there are crosses or circles on the chart, plus 1 extra treble.

How to work spaces

A space is usually made up of 2 chains plus a linking treble and is shown as an open space, □, on the chart. To remember this formula calculate 2 chains and 1 treble for each open space on the chart, plus 1 extra treble. The size of each space can be altered by working more or less chains between each linking treble, or by working a double crochet or half treble as the linking stitch, but if this is intended it is clearly stated in the instructions.

How to work lacets

A lacet is usually made up of 3 chains, a double crochet and a further 3 chains and is shown as a 'v' over 2 squares on the chart. Make 3 chains, miss 2 trebles of a block or 2 chains of a space in the previous row, work a double crochet into the next stitch, make 3 chains, miss the next 2 trebles or 2 chains in the previous row and work 1 treble into the next stitch to complete the lacet.

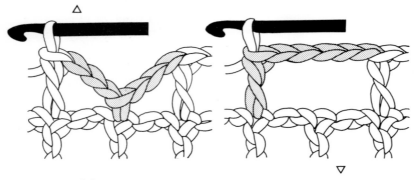

How to work bars

A bar is usually made up of 5 chains plus a linking treble and is shown as a dash, '–', over 2 squares on the chart. Make 5 chains then miss 5 stitches or 1 complete lacet in the previous row and work 1 treble into the next stitch to complete the bar.

Filet net background fabric

This requires a number of chains divisible by 3, plus 1 and 4 additional chains, e.g. 32 chains.

1st row (RS). Into 8th ch from hook work 1tr noting that the 7ch which have been missed form a 2ch space along the commencing edge, 3ch form the first tr and the last 2ch form a space on the row being worked, *2ch, miss 2ch, 1tr into next ch, rep from * to end. Turn.

2nd row. 5ch to count as first tr and 2ch space, miss first tr and 2ch space, 1tr into next tr, *2ch, miss 2ch space, 1tr into next tr, rep from * to end, working last tr into the 5th of the first 7ch. Turn.

3rd row. 5ch to count as first tr and 2ch space, miss first tr and 2ch space, 1tr into next tr, *2ch, miss 2ch space, 1tr into next tr, rep from * to end, working last tr into the 3rd of the first 5ch. Turn.

The 3rd row forms the pattern.

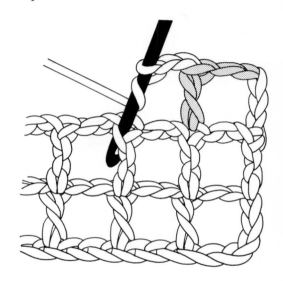

Working blocks into spaces

Blocks can be worked as required against a net background by making 1 treble into the corresponding treble of the previous row, then 2 treble into the next 2 chain space and a further treble into the next treble to complete a block of 3 trebles plus a linking treble.

Working blocks
into spaces

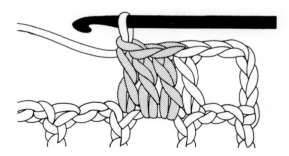

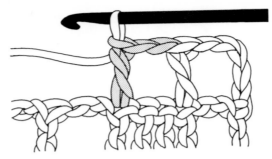

Working spaces over blocks △

Spaces can be worked by making 1 treble into the corresponding treble of the previous row, missing the next 2 trebles of the block and making 2 chains to form the space, then work a further treble into the next treble forming a 2 chain space with a linking treble on each side.

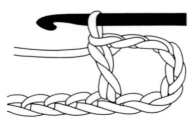

Beginning the 1st row with a block △

Miss 3 chains to count as the first treble and work the 2nd treble of the 1st block into the 4th chain from the hook, then 1 treble into each of the next 2 chains to complete the block. The diagram for the cushion motif shown here requires a commencing chain of 93 and begins with a row of 30 blocks.

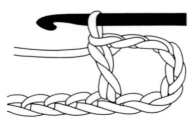

Beginning the 1st row with a space △

Miss 7 chains to count as a 2 chain space along the lower edge, the first treble and a further 2 chain space on the row being worked, work

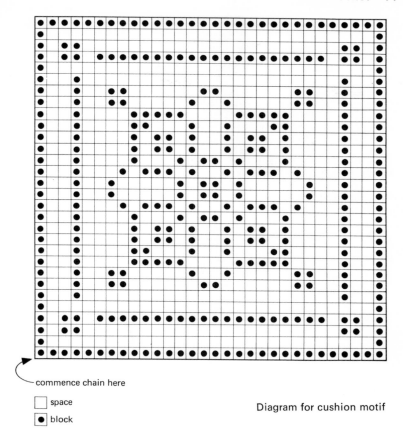

commence chain here

space
block

Diagram for cushion motif

the next treble into the 8th chain from the hook to complete the space.

Increasing in filet crochet

Where single increases are required at each end of a row, the continuity of the pattern must be maintained by means of an additional treble for the beginning of a new block, or 1 chain for the beginning of a new space, worked inside the turning chains (page 19).

To increase a complete block at the beginning of a row make 5 chains, work 1 treble into the 4th chain from hook, 1 treble into the next chain and 1 treble into the last stitch of the previous row to complete the block.

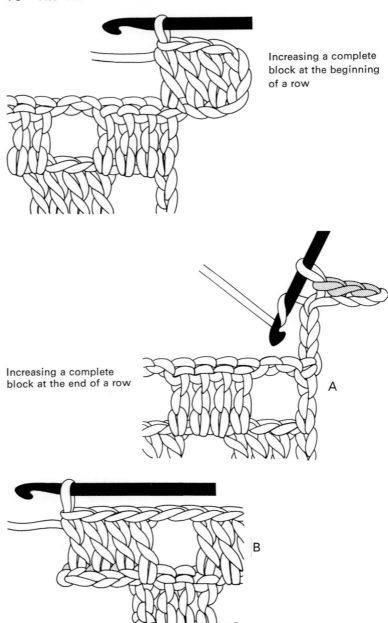

Increasing a complete block at the beginning of a row

Increasing a complete block at the end of a row

A

B

To increase a complete block at the end of a row, provision must be made for the increase at the beginning of the previous row by making 7 extra chains, miss the 1st chain and slip stitch across each of the next 3 chains, leaving the remaining 3 chains to count as the 1st treble of the row being worked. At the end of the row where the increase is required work the 1st treble into the 3rd of the 3 turning chains, then 1 treble into each of the 3 slip stitches to complete the block.

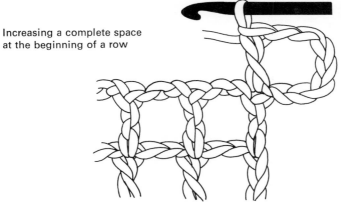

Increasing a complete space
at the beginning of a row

To increase a complete space at the beginning of a row make 7 chains, miss these chains and work the next treble into the last stitch of the previous row to complete the space.

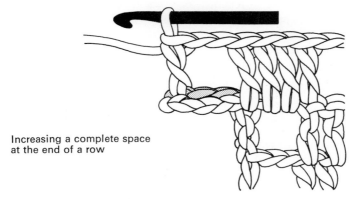

Increasing a complete space
at the end of a row

To increase a complete space at the end of a row work as given for increasing a block at the end of a row, working 1 treble into the 3rd of the 3 turning chains, make 2 chains and miss 2 slip stitches, then work 1 treble into the last slip stitch to complete the space.

Decreasing in filet crochet

Where single decreases are required at each end of a row, the continuity of the pattern must be maintained either by working 2 trebles together in a block, or making 1 chain less in a space, working the decreases inside the turning chains (page 19).

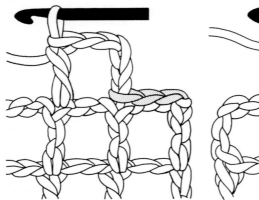

Decreasing a complete block or space at the beginning of a row

Decreasing a complete block or space at the end of a row

To decrease a block or space at the beginning of a row, slip stitch across each of the 1st 3 stitches and into the 4th, make 3 chains to count as the 1st treble of a block, or 5 chains to count as the 1st treble and 2 chain space of a space, then continue in pattern to the end.

To decrease a block or space at the end of a row, turn the work without working the last block or space and continue in pattern for the next row.

Cut looped fabric

Make the required area of filet net background, but using only 1 chain for each space and working half trebles instead of trebles for each linking stitch. Make a number of chains divisible by 2, plus 1 and 2 additional chains, e.g. 19 chains, working the 1st half treble into the 5th chain from the hook on the 1st row and beginning subsequent rows with 3 chains.

To work the loops, cut the yarn into lengths of approximately 12 cm, take two or more strands together and fold these in half.

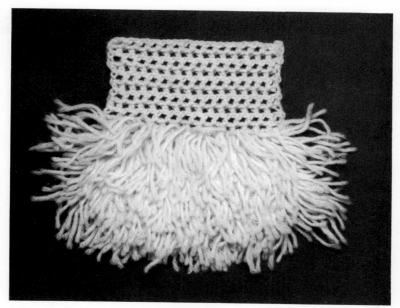

Working loops onto a filet net background

Have the right side of the background facing you and work in a vertical direction from the lower to the top edge, inserting the hook from the front under the first 1 chain space of the 1st row and out to the front again. Place the folded loops of yarn over the hook and pull these through the space, then place the cut ends of yarn over the hook and draw these through the loops on the hook, pulling them up tightly. This action can be repeated into every 1 chain space or alternate 1 chain space on every row, or alternate row, depending on the thickness of fabric required.

Woven fabric

Make a filet net background as given for cut looped fabric. Lengths of contrast coloured yarn should be cut to the same length as the background, allowing an extra amount of approximately 4 cm to each 10 cm to be taken up in weaving and turned under and secured at each end, or left free to form a fringed effect.

Have the right side of the background facing you and thread 2 or more strands of yarn into a blunt-ended wool needle. Begin at the

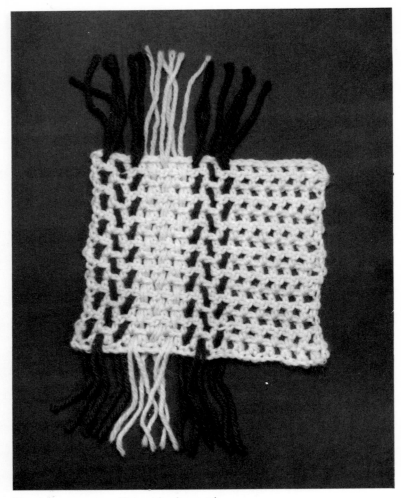

Weaving yarn onto a filet net background

lower right-hand edge of the net and thread the yarn under the first chain space in the 1st row and over the first chain space in the 2nd row, and continue in this way to the top right-hand edge. Begin again at the lower right-hand edge taking the yarn over the second chain space in the 1st row and under the second chain space in the 2nd row to alternate the position of the woven effect. Continue in this way until the entire area has been covered, varying the colours as required.

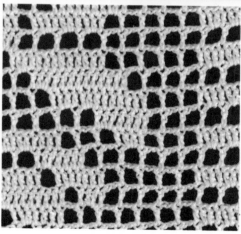

Filet crochet curtain
Designed by J & P Coats

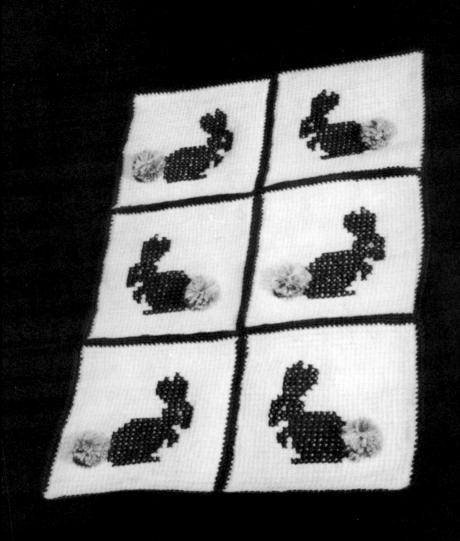

9 Tunisian crochet

This form of the craft is unique and links knitting to crochet in its working method and the appearance of some examples of the finished fabric. It comes into the category of crochet because it is worked with a single hooked tool but, with the exception of the commencing chains needed to produce the required width of fabric and a working loop on the hook, it does not resemble any other type of crochet.

The fabric is worked in pairs of rows, the first of them worked from right to left to build up a series of loops on the hook and the second worked back from left to right, reducing these loops until only the working loop remains. The height of each section of a row is very shallow so no additional chains are required to count as turning chains – 20 chains produce exactly 20 stitches. However, multiples of chains are needed to produce some patterns to ensure that each row works out correctly (page 43).

The right side of the work is always facing you as the rows are not turned, and the fabric achieved by this technique is very firm and hard-wearing. The fabric sometimes has a tendency to pull out of shape at the side edges. This biased effect can easily be overcome by working the stitches fairly loosely; when working the second section of a row take care not to pull the first stitch through too tightly thus throwing this edge out of true.

Tunisian crochet can be shaped by means of increasings and decreasings – either a single stitch or multiples of stitches at each end of a row or at any given point.

Plain Tunisian or Afghan stitch

This basic stitch will work out over any number of chains to give the width of fabric required.

Tunisian crochet pram cover in Hayfield Falkland
Designed by Jean Litchfield

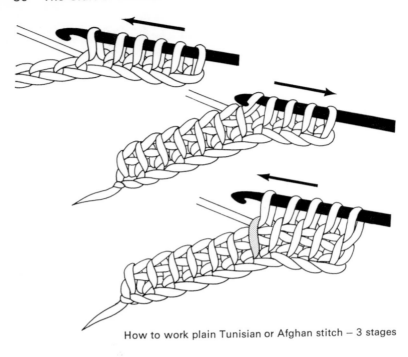

How to work plain Tunisian or Afghan stitch — 3 stages

Sample of plain Tunisian or Afghan stitch

Sample of Tunisian
stocking stitch

1st row (1st section). Miss the first ch, *insert hook into next ch, yrh and draw a loop through the ch keeping the loop on the hook, rep from * to end. Do not turn. The number of loops on the hook should be the same as the number of commencing chains.

1st row (2nd section). Yrh and draw a loop through the first loop on the hook keeping this fairly loose, *yrh and draw a loop through the next 2 loops on hook, rep from * until only the working loop remains on the hook. Do not turn.

2nd row (1st section). Miss the first vertical loop on the front of the work, *insert hook under the vertical loop of the next st from right to left, yrh and draw a loop through keeping the loop on the hook, rep from * to end. Do not turn. Check that the number of sts is correct as it is easy to miss the last st of this section.

2nd row (2nd section). As 2nd section of 1st row.

The 1st and 2nd sections of the 2nd row form the pattern which should end with a 2nd section of the row.

Tunisian stocking stitch

Make the required number of chains and work the 1st and 2nd sections of the 1st row as given for plain Tunisian stitch.

2nd row (1st section). *Insert hook from the front to the back into the centre of the next 2 vertical loops of the next st on the previous row, yrh and draw a loop through loosely keeping the loop on the hook, rep from * to end. Do not turn. Check the number of sts.

2nd row (2nd section). As 2nd section of 2nd row of Tunisian st.

The 1st and 2nd sections of the 2nd row form the pattern which should end with a 2nd section of the row.

Tunisian eyelet stitch

Make a number of chains divisible by 4, e.g. 24 chains.

1st row (1st section). As 1st section of 1st row of plain Tunisian st.

1st row (2nd section). Yrh and draw through first 2 loops on hook fairly loosely, *make 4ch for eyelet, yrh and draw through 5 loops on hook, rep from * to last 3 loops on hook, make 3ch for last eyelet, yrh and draw through 3 loops on hook, make 1ch loosely. Do not turn.

Sample of Tunisian eyelet stitch

2nd row (1st section). (Insert hook into next ch of eyelet, yrh and draw a loop through keeping loop on hook) 3 times, *(insert hook into next ch of eyelet, yrh and draw a loop through keeping loop on hook) 4 times, rep from * to end. Do not turn. Check the number of sts.

2nd row (2nd section). As 2nd section of 1st row.

The 1st and 2nd sections of the 2nd row form the pattern which should end with the 2nd section of the 2nd row but working 3ch for each eyelet instead of 4ch.

Tunisian treble stitch

Make any number of chains.

1st row (1st section). 1ch, yrh, insert hook into 3rd ch from hook, yrh and draw loop through ch, yrh and draw through 2 loops on hook, *yrh, insert hook into next ch, yrh and draw loop through ch, yrh and draw through 2 loops on hook, rep from * to end. Do not turn.

Sample of Tunisian treble stitch

1st row (2nd section). As 2nd section of 1st row of plain Tunisian st.

2nd row (1st section). 1ch, miss the first vertical loop on the front of the work, *yrh, insert hook under the vertical loop of the next st from right to left, yrh and draw a loop through, yrh and draw through 2 loops on hook, rep from * to end. Do not turn. Check the number of sts.

2nd row (2nd section). As 2nd section of 1st row.

The 1st and 2nd sections of the 2nd row form the pattern which should end with the 2nd section of the row.

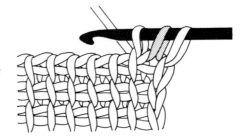

Increasing one stitch
at the beginning of a row

Increasing in Tunisian crochet

A single stitch can be increased at each end of the 1st section of a row. At the beginning of the row insert the hook under the horizontal loop which lies between the 1st 2 vertical loops and draw a loop through, keeping this loop on the hook to form an extra stitch. At the end of a row insert the hook under the horizontal loop lying between the last and last but one vertical loops and draw a loop through to increase 1 stitch.

A single stitch can also be increased at any given point in the 1st section of a row in the same way, working the increased stitch under the horizontal loop which lies between the vertical loops and drawing an extra loop through on to the hook.

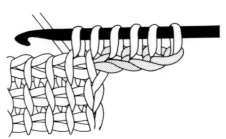

Increasing extra stitches
at the beginning of a row

Extra stitches can be increased at the beginning of the 1st section of a row by making the number of chains required to give the number of extra stitches, miss the 1st chain, pick up a loop into each of the remaining chains then continue in pattern to the end.

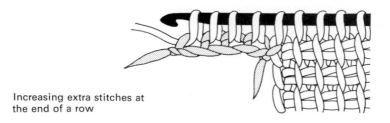

Increasing extra stitches at
the end of a row

Extra stitches can be increased at the end of the 1st section of a row by working to the end of this row, make the number of chains required to give the number of extra stitches with a spare length of matching yarn and join this with a slip stitch to the last loop of the row, then pick up a loop into each of these chains with the main yarn.

Decreasing one stitch
at the beginning of a row

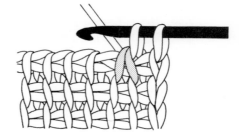

Decreasing in Tunisian crochet

A single stitch can be decreased at each end of the 1st section of a row. At the beginning of the row miss the 1st vertical loop on the front of the work, insert the hook under the 2nd and 3rd vertical loops from right to left and work these 2 loops together to form 1 loop. At the end of the row insert the hook under the last 2 vertical loops before the last loop and work these 2 loops together, then work the last loop.

A single stitch can also be decreased at any given point in the 1st section of a row in the same way, working the decreased stitch under 2 vertical loops to form 1 loop.

To decrease several stitches at the beginning of the 1st section of a row, slip stitch over the required number of stitches to be decreased and continue in pattern to the end of this section of the row.

To decrease several stitches at the end of the 1st section of a row, work in pattern until the number of stitches to be decreased remain, leave these stitches unworked and complete the 2nd section of the row.

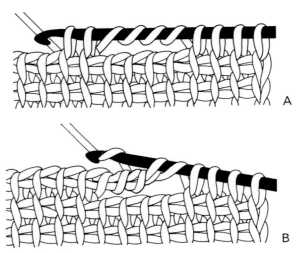

Making a buttonhole in Tunisian crochet – 2 stages

Making a buttonhole in Tunisian crochet

The buttonhole is made on the 1st section of a row. Work in pattern until the position for the buttonhole is reached, wind the yarn round the hook for the required number of stitches for the buttonhole and miss this number of stitches in the previous row, then continue in pattern to the end.

On the 2nd section of this row draw a loop through each of the loops wound round the hook for the buttonhole as if it were a stitch.

10 Hairpin crochet

This method was originally worked literally on a wire hairpin to produce an exquisitely delicate edging for a handkerchief, collar and cuffs or on any item where a fine lace trimming was required. Although this type of work was very beautiful, it was also extremely tedious and the technique has been modified to make it more practical for adaptation to modern tastes.

Hairpin prongs are available in various widths (page 15) so that individual strips can be worked and then joined together to form an all-over fabric suitable for shawls, cushions or complete garments. A crochet hook of a size suitable for the yarn being used is needed to secure the loops round the prong and most basic crochet stitches can be worked to form a central linking panel on each strip. Almost any type of yarn can be used from the very finest cotton or rayon to soft, bulky combinations of fibres but, because the strips are very open and lacy, it is not advisable to work with a heavy yarn which would tend to drop out of shape.

Once the strips have been completed the free loops on either side can be plaited or crocheted together in many different ways, or an edging can be worked along one side of a strip to complete a section neatly.

How to begin a basic strip

There are two ways of working the basic strips and it is largely a question of preference as to which method is used.

First method

Hold the prong in the shape of a 'U' with the open ends at the top. Make a slip loop in the usual way and put this on the right-hand rod of the prong. Draw the loop out so that the knot is central between the two rods. Hold the main end of yarn behind the left-hand rod

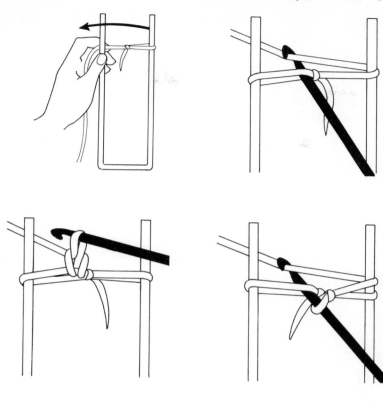

1st method for working a basic strip

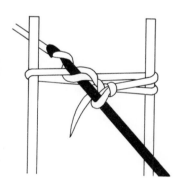

Lampshade in hairpin crochet
Designed by J & P Coats

with the left hand, then turn the prong towards you from right to left until the right-hand rod is in position on the left-hand side. The yarn should again be held behind the left-hand rod with the left hand.

Hold the crochet hook in the right hand and insert it into the front loop on the left-hand rod, put the main end of yarn over the hook and draw a loop through on to the hook, yarn round hook and draw through the loop on the hook to make a slip stitch.

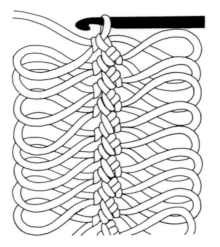

Loops are twisted when removed from the prong

*Keep this loop on the hook and take the hook over the top of and behind the right-hand rod, then turn the prong towards you from right to left as before. The stitch which has just been worked is now on the right-hand rod. Hold the yarn behind the left-hand rod with the left hand. Insert the crochet hook into the front of the top loop on the left-hand rod, yarn round hook and draw a loop through on to the hook, yarn round hook and draw through both loops on hook. One double crochet has been worked to secure the loops. Continue in this way from the point marked with an asterisk until the prong is filled with loops. Slip all the loops off the prong and replace the last 3 or 4 loops worked in the correct order on to the rods, then continue until the prong is filled again. It should be noted that as the loops are taken off the prong, each one will be twisted.

Second method

Hold the prong in the shape of an inverted 'U', the open ends at the bottom. Work as given for the first method until the slip loop is completed.

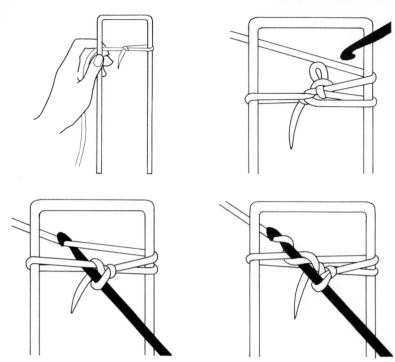

2nd method for working a strip

*Remove the hook from the working loop and turn the prong towards you from right to left as before. Replace the hook into the working loop. The stitch which has just been worked is now on the right-hand rod. Hold the yarn behind the left-hand rod with the left hand. Insert the crochet hook into the front of the top loop on the left-hand rod, yarn round hook and draw a loop through on to the hook, yarn round hook and draw through both loops on hook. One double crochet has been worked to secure the loops. Continue in this way from the point marked with an asterisk for the required length, allowing the loops to drop off the rods as the prong is filled. The loops will also be twisted (see first method).

To finish off each strip, break off the yarn and draw it through the last stitch, then pull it up tightly to secure.

Variations in strips

The width and density of the central linking panel of the loops can be altered in various ways.

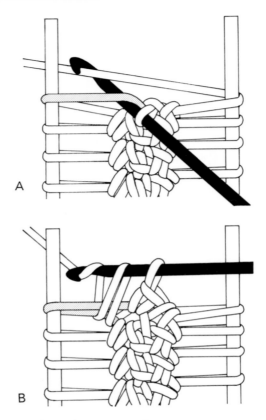

Working two double crochets to secure loops

Working two double crochets

Work the first double crochet as for the basic strip into the front of the loop, then work a second double crochet under both threads of the loop before turning the prong.

Working trebles

Work as given for the basic method until the first slip loop has been completed.

   *Before working the next stitch take the yarn across the top of the hook and hold it in place with the index finger of the right hand, insert the hook into the front loop on the left-hand rod, yarn round hook and draw a loop through (3 loops on hook), yarn round hook

Yarn across hook to begin
a treble

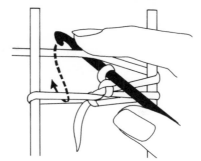

and draw through 2 loops on hook (2 loops on hook), yarn round
hook and draw through both loops on hook. One treble has been
completed. Continue from the point marked with an asterisk, as
required.

Two trebles can be worked into each loop, working the second
stitch under both threads of the loop before turning the prong.

Working half trebles

Work as given for trebles until there are 3 loops on the hook, yarn
round the hook and draw through all 3 loops on hook. One half
treble has been completed.

Two half trebles can be worked, as given for trebles.

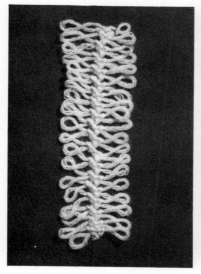

Working a treble to secure loops

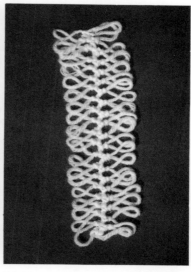

Working half trebles to secure loops

Joining the strips

Once the required number of strips have been completed, the way in which they are joined and the number of loops taken together give this technique great scope. To ensure that the existing twist of each loop remains in the correct position when joining strips together, the crochet hook must be inserted through the loop from the bottom to the top on the right-hand edge of the strip and from the top to the bottom on the left-hand edge. This principle applies whether 1, 2 or more loops are to be joined by any of the following methods. To untwist each loop to give a more open effect to the strip, simply reverse this procedure.

To begin joining the strips together place them side by side in a vertical direction and work from the left-hand edge of the right-hand strip, referred to as the 1st strip, across to the right-hand edge of the left-hand strip, referred to as the 2nd strip.

Simple plaited join

Pick up the 1st loop of the 1st strip with a crochet hook, then pick up the corresponding loop on the 2nd strip and pull this loop through the loop on the hook. Pick up the 2nd loop of the 1st strip and pull

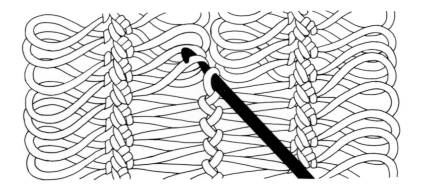

this through the loop on the hook, then pick up the next loop of the 2nd strip and pull this through the loop on the hook. Continue in this way until all the loops of both strips are joined together, then securely sew the last loop in place to prevent the edge unravelling.

This method can also be used to pick up 2 or more loops at a time to form a heavier join.

Chain stitch join

This method requires a separate ball of yarn for joining. Make a slip loop in the ball of yarn and place this on a crochet hook and hold the yarn at the back of the work throughout. *Insert the hook into

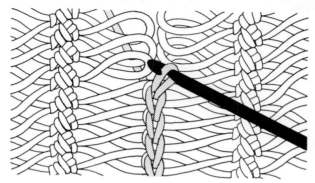

the 1st loop of the 1st strip then into the 1st loop of the 2nd strip, yarn round hook and draw a loop through the 3 loops on the hook. Repeat from the point marked with an asterisk until all the loops are joined together, break off the yarn and pull it through the last stitch to fasten off.

This method can also be used to pick up two or more loops at a time to form a heavier join.

Faggoting join

A separate ball of yarn is also required for this method. Make a slip loop in the ball of yarn and place this on a crochet hook, holding

Faggoting join

Sewn join

the yarn at the back of the work throughout. *Insert the hook into the first 3 loops of the 1st strip and work 1dc, 3ch, insert the hook into the first 3 loops of the 2nd strip and work 1dc, 3ch, repeat from * into each group of 3 loops to the end, omitting 3ch at the end of the last repeat. Break off the yarn and fasten off.

Sewn join

In this method the outer edges of each strip are neatened and held in place with crochet, then the strips can be oversewn together. This method requires a separate ball of yarn.

Make a slip loop in the ball of yarn and place this on a crochet hook. Working from right to left along one long edge of the strip, *insert the hook into the first 4 loops and work 1dc, 5ch, *, rep from * to * into each group of 4 loops to end, omitting 5ch at end of last rep, **make the number of ch needed to reach to the centre panel across the short end, work 2dc into the end of the centre panel then make the same number of ch to reach the outer edge of the strip, **, rep from * to * along the other long edge of the strip omitting 5ch at the end of the last rep, work from ** to ** across other short end. Join with a ss to first dc. Fasten off.

To finish an unjoined edge

However many strips are joined together to form a flat section the first and last strips have an unfinished edge which needs to be neatened to complete the fabric. If a single strip is required as an edging it also needs to be completed in the same way.

Double crochet edging

Make a slip loop in a ball of yarn and place this on a hook. Working from right to left along the edge of the strip, *insert the hook into the first loop, yarn round hook and draw a loop through, yarn round hook and draw through both loops on hook to form 1dc, rep from * to end. Break off yarn and fasten off. Work other edge in same way.

When working this edging where trebles have been used as the centre linking panel of the strip, work one double crochet into each loop with one chain between each stitch to avoid pulling the edge up too tightly.

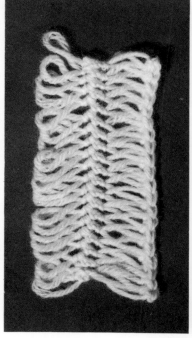
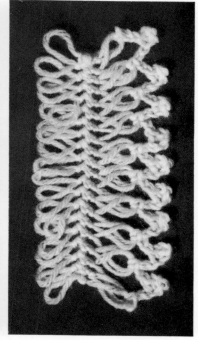

Double crochet edging   Picot edging

Cushion in hairpin crochet
Designed by J & P Coats

Picot edging

Make a slip loop in a ball of yarn and place this on a hook. Working from right to left along the edge of the strip, insert the hook into the first 2 loops and work 1dc, *make 6ch, into 4th ch from hook work 1dc, 2ch, work 1dc into next 2 loops, rep from * to end. Break off yarn and fasten off. Work other edge in same way.

Sewn-on edging

Where a strip is to be used as a lace trimming one side of the loops can be left free and the other side should be neatened to form a sewing edge.

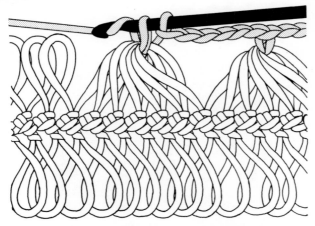

Make a slip loop in a ball of yarn and place this on a hook. Working from right to left along the edge of the strip, insert the hook into the first 6 loops and work 1dc, *make 6ch, insert hook into next 6 loops and work 1dc, rep from * to end. Break off yarn and fasten off.

11 Basic designing

To begin any design you need to know the exact size and shape of the item you have in mind and the tension you obtain with the yarn and hook size of your choice (page 13); simple mathematics will take care of the rest. When you design for yourself you are no longer restricted to working to the same tension as another person but can experiment to produce the effect you require.

There are certain points which must be taken into account, however, particularly when planning a garment or any item where the measurements have to be accurate – a wall hanging or afghan can be to any shape or size so accurate measurements are not so vital. You need to know your own tension, so a sample is still required on which all your calculations will be based. Take into account the type of item you have in mind – do you want a soft, delicate effect or a tough, hardwearing fabric and choose your yarn, hook size and stitch accordingly.

Body measurements

Begin with your own exact body measurements, calculating the width and length of each section of the garment. The chart overleaf gives the 'average' basic measurements for knitted and crocheted garments but does not take into account an additional amount for ease of movement or 'tolerance', or individual measurements such as shoulders, neck, wrist and so on.

These sizes cannot be compared with those of a ready-to-wear garment where the tolerance has been taken into account and they are only given as a guide to those measurements most widely used. If you are unusually short or tall, short- or long-waisted, large-busted or long-armed, then designing for yourself very often proves to be the only satisfactory way of ensuring a perfect fit.

Hooded crochet coat using hand-dyed yarn
Designed by Rosemary Cassidy, graduate of the Manchester College of Art

Average metric measurements for knitted or crochet garments
(not allowing for tolerance)

	age or size	chest or bust (cm)	waist (cm)	hips (cm)	upper arm (cm)	arm-hole (cm)	sleeve length (cm)
babies	birth	42			14	8	12
	6 months	45			16	9	15
	1 year	48			18	10	18
	18 months	51			20	11	21
children	2 years	55			21	11	21
	3 years	57			22	12	24
	4 years	60			23	13	27
	6 years	65			25	14	30
	8 years	70			27	15	33
	10 years	75			30	17	37
	12 years	80			33	18	41
women	size 10	80	60	86	33	19	42
	size 12	85	65	90	34	20	42
	size 14	90	70	96	35	21	43
	size 16	96	75	101	36	21	44
	size 18	101	80	106	37	22	45
	size 20	106	85	111	38	23	46
men	size 91	90/96			40	23	47
	size 97	96/101			41	24	48
	size 102	101/106			42	25	49
	size 107	106/111			43	26	50
	size 112	111/116			44	27	51

Once you have taken a note of your exact measurements you need to calculate an extra amount of tolerance. An overall width measurement of approximately 5 cm is usually sufficient but, obviously, any garment which is going to be worn over another will need more ease of movement than a figure-hugging T-shirt. The best way to solve this is to use an existing garment of the type you have in mind which is a good fit and measure this to see how much tolerance has been allowed.

Planning the shape

Based on the measurements you have obtained you should now decide on the exact shape of each section of the garment and the individual details such as pockets, front opening, high or low neck, long or short sleeves and put all this information down on paper in rough sketch form with a note of all the measurements. Add to this such details as how many buttons will be needed, the pattern rows of the stitch you have selected, the position of pockets and so on.

The body and sleeve diagrams shown here are for a basic jersey shape and should be used as a guide for this step.

Diagram 1

The centre line from the points marked A to B shows the total length from the lower edge to the centre back neck. Points marked C to D show the lower edge measurement of the back, E to F the waist measurement, G to H the bust measurement and J and K the back neck and shoulder measurements.

Diagram 2

The centre line from the points marked L to M shows the sleeve measurement from the cuff to shoulder, from N to P the sleeve seam measurement. Points marked N to O show the wrist measurement and P to Q the upper-arm measurement.

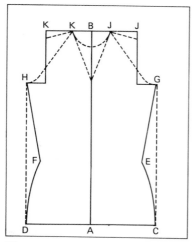

Diagram 1 – body measurements

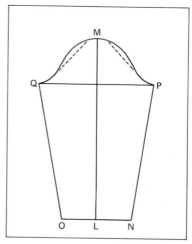

Diagram 2 – sleeve measurements

Armhole shaping

The shaping should be worked in the first 4 to 7 cm above the points marked G to H on Diagram 1, the curve being more acute at the beginning then tapering to a gradual curve for a set-in sleeve, or continuing until the required width of the back neck remains for a raglan sleeve.

Shoulder shaping

For a set-in sleeve the shoulder shaping should begin approximately 1 to 3 cm below the total length given from A to B on Diagram 1.

Raglan sleeves do not need any shoulder shaping as the head of the sleeve forms the shoulder line.

Sleeve shaping

The arm of a sleeve will probably need to be increased at regular intervals from the wrist measurement, N to O on Diagram 2, to the upper-arm measurement, P to Q on Diagram 2.

The head of a set-in sleeve must be shaped in a curve to match the armhole shaping on the body then decreased to leave a width of approximately 6 to 12 cm at a point approximately 1 to 3 cm below the total length required from points marked L to M on Diagram 2. The remaining stitches should be sharply decreased at the beginning of the next few rows until a width of approximately 3 to 7 cm remains and the correct overall length has been reached.

The head of a raglan sleeve must match the armhole shaping on the body, making sure that the sleeve fits without stretching along the raglan edges of the body. Sufficient stitches should be left to form the side neck edge.

Neck shaping

The centre back neck can be left as a straight line once the shoulder shaping has been completed, or the work can be divided and a slightly curved neck worked in with the shoulder shaping.

The position for the centre front neck shaping will depend on the type of neckline required but, as a general guide, the shaping for a round neck should begin approximately 4 to 7 cm below the back neck. The work is divided at this point and each section worked separately. The stitches needed to complete each shoulder for a set-in

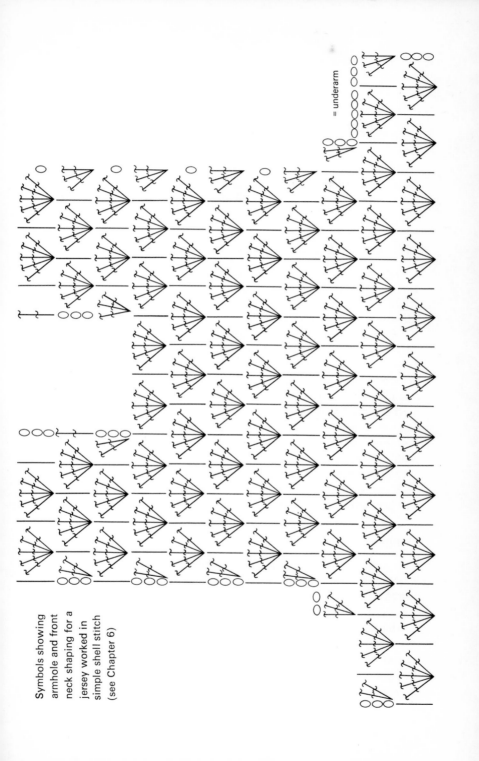

= underarm

Symbols showing armhole and front neck shaping for a jersey worked in simple shell stitch (see Chapter 6)

sleeve should be deducted from the total number of stitches and the remaining stitches decreased in a gradual curve before beginning the shoulder shaping, or until all the stitches have been decreased for a raglan sleeve.

A V-necked jersey is usually divided, or the front neck shaping of a cardigan commenced at the same point as the armhole shaping, or after the armhole shaping has been completed, depending on the depth of neck required. The stitches should be decreased at regular intervals until the stitches needed to complete the shoulder for a set-in sleeve remain, or until all stitches have been decreased for a raglan sleeve.

Planning the fabric

Using the number of stitches and rows you have obtained with a given yarn and hook size, you must now calculate the number of stitches and rows required to achieve the measurements, including tolerance, of your design.

As a guide, say you are working in rows of trebles at a tension of 16 stitches and 10 rows to 10 cm and the commencing width of the back of a jersey is 45 cm. If you place a decimal point between the number of stitches and rows, thus, 1·6 and 1·0, this gives you the exact number to 1 centimetre. Now multiply the stitch figure of 1·6 by the width figure of 45, and you arrive at the total of 72 stitches to begin this section. The number of rows required to reach the under-arm and complete the back should now be calculated in the same way.

Using a piece of lined paper and the symbols given on page 28, work out a diagram of each section, taking any necessary shaping into account and use this as a pattern.

Multiples of stitches

Unless you are working in a basic stitch such as trebles, you must take into account the multiples of stitches plus any edge stitches required to make the pattern work out exactly (see chapter 6, page 43).

Taking the previous example of 72 stitches to give the correct width and a pattern which requires multiples of 6 plus 4 edge stitches, you will see that this will not divide exactly into the total. Twelve repeats of the pattern total 72 stitches and a further 4 are needed for the edge stitches, making 76 stitches. Eleven repeats of the pattern total 66 stitches and a further 4 make 70 stitches. You must now decide whether to reduce or increase the total to ensure that you have the correct multiples.

Calculating the yarn required

Yarn varies enormously in its construction and, because it is sold by weight and not by length, each individual quality also varies in the amount contained in each ball.

The only way to arrive at the total amount required for a design is to purchase one ball to begin with of the quality you have selected and work as far as you can with this ball across the total number of stitches. You are then able to calculate how many balls are needed to complete each section and arrive at a total. As an example, say you are working over 72 trebles and the depth required to complete this section is 60 cm. If one ball works 10 cm over this number of stitches, then a total of 6 balls will complete the section.

Do remember to allow for shaping and any separate trimmings such as pockets, neckbands, front bands, etc., in your calculations. Because it is difficult to obtain the exact dye lot at a later date it is better to over-estimate rather than under-estimate.

12 The final touches

With the possible exception of incorrect tension, more garments are probably ruined at the making-up stage than by any other cause. Meticulous attention to the details of pressing, seaming, applying edges or any other trimmings makes the difference between a highly successful hand-made garment and a depressingly cobbled home-made attempt.

Don't be in too much of a hurry to complete and wear a garment. Because crochet is very quick to work you may well be able to complete all the sections of a garment in a few days – you should spend almost as much time on assembling the pieces.

Pressing and after-care
Most of the branded yarns available today are wound into balls and each ball is secured with a paper band, referred to as a 'ball band'. This band contains a wealth of information, such as the weight of the ball, the composition of the yarn, the colour and dye lot numbers and laundering and pressing details.

The correct way to handle a yarn is of vital importance if all your efforts are not to be wasted at the final making-up stage. The Home Laundering Consultative Council has compiled a list of symbols relating to pressing, washing and dry cleaning. The codes applying to any particular yarn are usually shown on the ball band; you should check these very carefully before beginning to make up any design.

The following list can be used as a general guide to pressing and in cases where blends of different fibres have been used to produce a certain yarn, such as wool and nylon, check which fibre has the highest content and adopt the procedure recommended for this. It is never advisable to press any acrylic yarn.

Wool: press under a damp cloth with a warm iron.

Cotton: press under a damp cloth with a warm or hot iron.

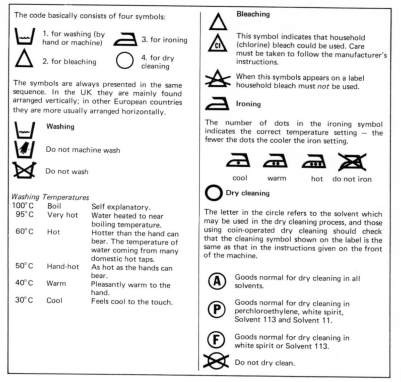

The code basically consists of four symbols:

1. for washing (by hand or machine)
2. for bleaching
3. for ironing
4. for dry cleaning

The symbols are always presented in the same sequence. In the UK they are mainly found arranged vertically; in other European countries they are more usually arranged horizontally.

Washing

Do not machine wash

Do not wash

Washing Temperatures

100°C	Boil	Self explanatory.
95°C	Very hot	Water heated to near boiling temperature.
60°C	Hot	Hotter than the hand can bear. The temperature of water coming from many domestic hot taps.
50°C	Hand-hot	As hot as the hands can bear.
40°C	Warm	Pleasantly warm to the hand.
30°C	Cool	Feels cool to the touch.

Bleaching

This symbol indicates that household (chlorine) bleach could be used. Care must be taken to follow the manufacturer's instructions.

When this symbols appears on a label household bleach must *not* be used.

Ironing

The number of dots in the ironing symbol indicates the correct temperature setting — the fewer the dots the cooler the iron setting.

cool   warm   hot   do not iron

Dry cleaning

The letter in the circle refers to the solvent which may be used in the dry cleaning process, and those using coin-operated dry cleaning should check that the cleaning symbol shown on the label is the same as that in the instructions given on the front of the machine.

(A) Goods normal for dry cleaning in all solvents.

(P) Goods normal for dry cleaning in perchloroethylene, white spirit, Solvent 113 and Solvent 11.

(F) Goods normal for dry cleaning in white spirit or Solvent 113.

Do not dry clean.

List of pressing, washing and dry cleaning symbols

Acrylic: do not press.

Courtelle: do not press.

Nylon: press under a dry cloth with a cool iron, if directed.

Tricel: do not press.

Mohair: steam very lightly with a warm iron.

Lurex: do not press unless otherwise stated.

Where pressing has been recommended each section should be pinned out in turn, right side down, on to a large, well-padded surface, to the exact measurements stated. This is referred to as 'blocking'. It is essential to see that all the stitches and rows run in straight lines and that the side edges are not pulled out of shape. Use plenty of pins to secure each section.

Once the section has been pinned out have a clean piece of damp or dry cloth available and the iron at the recommended heat. Place

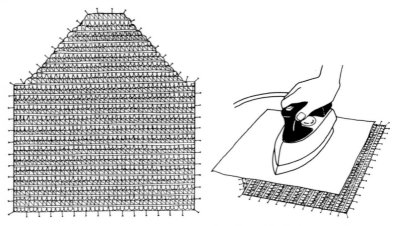

Blocking out a section   Pressing a blocked out section

the cloth over the section, then press the whole surface of the iron down on to the cloth, lift it, then place it down again to press the next area. The iron should not be moved across the entire area of the section, as you would when ironing, but lifted and pressed down again for each area. When the pressing has been completed, allow the section to cool, then remove the pins and put this piece aside until all the sections have been completed.

After-care

Where washing has been recommended a few simple hints will avoid the possibility of a ruined garment.

Use a mild soap or detergent powder especially recommended for knitwear. A fabric conditioner can be added to the final rinse to restore bulk to the fibres.

Avoid very hot water.

Never lift or handle a garment excessively when it is saturated with water. Gently squeeze out as much excess moisture as possible before handling.

Rinse very thoroughly using as many changes of water as are necessary. Insufficient rinsing results in a scum on the surface of the fibres and the eventual deterioration of the yarn.

Do not dry near any direct heat or in strong sunlight. Pad a kitchen table with old newspapers, then cover these with a clean towel. Place the garment on the towel, pat it gently into the correct size and shape, and leave it until all excess moisture has been removed.

To finish drying a garment put it over a line outdoors, pegging it lightly at the underarms. Never hang from the shoulders or from the waist.

Seaming

Two methods of seaming are suitable for crochet, flat and oversewn. Work as near to the edge as possible, taking care not to split the yarn. When joining the last rows of two sections to form a seam, take care to go under both loops at the top of the stitches on both pieces to avoid a ridge on the right side. Use a blunt-ended wool needle.

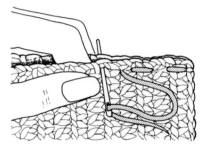

Flat seam

Have the right sides of the sections to be joined facing each other and secure the sewing yarn to one end. Place your forefinger between the two pieces and work from right to left along the edge. Push the needle through one piece directly across to the corresponding stitch on the other piece, and pull the yarn through. Turn the needle and move along to the next stitch, then push the needle back again and across to the matching stitch on the first piece and pull the yarn through. Continue in this way until the seam has been completed then fasten off the yarn securely.

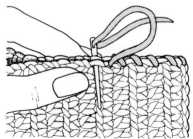

Oversewn seam

Have the right sides of the sections to be joined facing each other and secure the sewing yarn to the end of the uppermost section, working along the edge from right to left. Take the yarn over the top of both edges and insert the needle from the back into the first stitch on the underside section, push the needle through this stitch and the corresponding stitch on the uppermost section and pull the yarn through. Move along to the next stitch, take the yarn over the top again, insert the needle into the next stitch from the back, push the needle through this stitch and the corresponding stitch on the uppermost section and pull the yarn through. Continue in this way until the seam has been completed then fasten off the yarn securely.

Picking up stitches

Where a neckband or front bands have to be picked up after the sections have been seamed and completed separately, the stitches must be picked up evenly to avoid a cobbled effect. Prepare the edge by marking out 2 or 5 cm sections with pins, then pick up the same number of stitches between each pin.

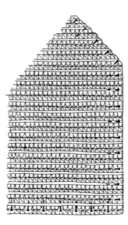

Pinning out an edge to pick up stitches

To pick up the stitches have the right side of the edge facing, the hook in your right hand and the yarn in your left hand. Insert the hook from front to back, either under both loops at the top of a stitch or into the turning chain or stitch at the end of a row, make a slip loop in the yarn and place this on the hook, then pull this loop through the edge. Make the required number of turning chains to form the first stitch, then continue working in pattern along the edge as required.

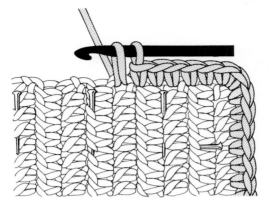

Picking up stitches along an edge

Trimmings

A completed garment may still require the final, finishing touch, such as a fringe or pompon. Always keep any oddments of yarn left over from a design to refurbish an old garment and give it a new lease of life.

Knotted fringing

Cut the yarn to twice the length of the finished fringe and use two or more strands together, depending on the thickness required. The

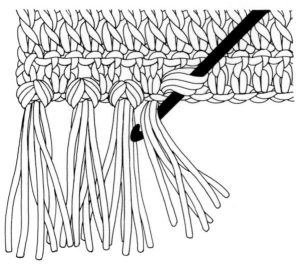

wrong side of the edge to be fringed should be facing you. Push a crochet hook through the edge of the fabric from the front to the back, fold the strands of yarn in half and place the folded loops on the hook. Pull the hook and loops through to the front, then put all the loose ends of the yarn round the hook again and pull them through the loops on the hook. Repeat along the edge into every stitch or alternate stitch as required.

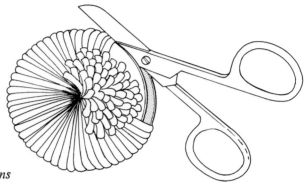

Pompons

You need two pieces of strong cardboard cut into circles with a smaller circle cut in the centre of each piece. The diameter of the larger circle determines the size of the finished pompon. Hold the two circles together and wind the yarn evenly round and through the centre hole, bringing in as many different oddments of yarn as you have available, until the hole is nearly filled. Thread the yarn into a blunt-ended sewing needle and use this to fill the hole completely.

Insert the point of a sharp pair of scissors between the two circles of cardboard at the outer edge and cut through all of the yarn. Tie a matching length of yarn securely round all the threads between the two circles leaving an end long enough to sew the pompon to the garment. Pull away the pieces of card then trim the pompon into shape.

Twisted cords

Cut the yarn into three times the length of the finished cord and use four or more strands together, depending on the thickness of the cord required and the type of yarn being used. Two people should each take one end of the strands and knot them together. Insert the un-shaped end of a crochet hook, or pencil, behind each knot; then, holding the strands taut, twist them in a clockwise direction until the twists run tightly and smoothly along the entire length. Keeping the strands taut throughout, fold them in half at the centre and knot the two ends together. Hold this knot, release the strands, give them a sharp shake, then smooth the cord from the knot to the folded end to even out the twists. Make a knot at the folded end and cut through the folded loops to complete the cord.

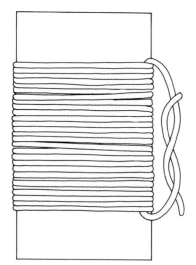

Tassels

Cut a piece of thin card the width of the finished length of the tassel. The card should be approximately twice as long as it is wide. Wind a continuous length of yarn round and round the card for the required thickness. Thread a blunt-ended sewing needle with a matching length of yarn. Insert the needle along one edge of the card under all the strands of yarn, pull the yarn through and fasten the two ends tightly and securely round the strands. Leave an end of yarn long enough to wind several times round the top, folded end of the tassel to complete it. Cut through all the strands of yarn on the other edge of the card and trim the tassel.

Crab stitch edging

With the right side of the work facing, work one row of double crochet along the edge to be trimmed in the usual way, working from

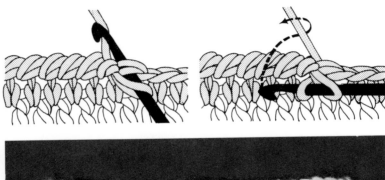

Crab stitch edging

right to left. Do not turn at the end of this row. Begin again and work another row of double crochet back along the first row from left to right. Fasten off.

Zigzag braid

Make 3ch.

1st row. Into the 3rd ch from hook work 1tr and 1dc. Turn.

2nd row. 2ch, into the dc of the previous row work 1tr and 1dc. Turn. Repeat the 2nd row for the length of braid required. Fasten off.

Zigzag braid

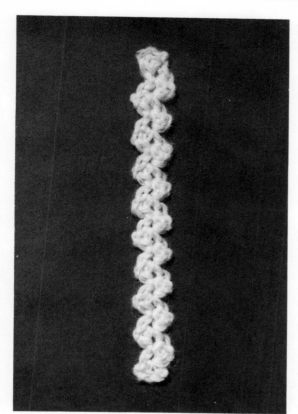

Index

Compiled by Kate Hibbert

$\sqrt{}\ \dfrac{12}{2}\ \dfrac{0,-}{1,No.}$